Oil Spills, Mafia Oil & Mafia Politics

How Congress and Oilmen betrayed the American People, an essay on American History

Giuseppe Ayroldi

Of the same author:
"L'Inquinamento d'oro, come si ruba - anche - sull'emergenza ambientale"

© 2016 LE VESPE, Roma
First Edition, May 2016
www. mafiaoil.com
levespeedizioni@gmail.com
ISBN 978-88-904440-2-9

"Politics is really shaped by interactions between elected governments and élites that overwhelmingly represent business interests."

Colin Crouch

"The devil must be an optimist if he thinks he can make men any worse than they are."

Karl Kraus

CONCRETE JUNGLE

No sun will shine in my day today
The high yellow moon won't come out to play
I said darkness has covered my light,
And has changed my day into night, yeah.
Where is the love to be found?
Won't someone tell me 'cause
Life must be somewhere to be found
Instead of concrete jungle,
I said where the living is hardest.
Concrete jungle
Man, you got to do your best
Wo-ooh

No chains around my feet
But I'm not free
I know I am bounded in captivity; oh now
Never known what happiness is;
I've never known what sweet caress is yeah
Still, I'll be always laughing like a clown;
Oh someone help me 'cause
I've got to pick myself from off the ground
In this ya concrete jungle:
I said, what do you got for me now?
Concrete jungle, why won't you let me be now?
Ohhh yeah

I said that life must be somewhere to be found
Oh, instead: concrete jungle - collusion -
Confusion. Eh!

Concrete jungle: we've made it, We've got it.
In Concrete jungle, now. Eh!
Concrete jungle.

What, what do you got for me now?

Bob Marley

CONTENTS

11

spills to the «thoroughly incompetent and devoid of adequate organization in the sector» Ecolmare Company

FOREWORD

This book is the result of four year's work. It took that long partly because they were difficult years for me and partly because I wanted to assure my kind readers that the dirty story I was about to tell was true, without boring them with long diatribes of the kind normally heard in courts of law (without having to continually say "they did this this and this and here is the evidence").

However, I constantly found myself back at the starting point. Every time, in fact, I had to prove what I said. And so it was that, after so many failed attempts and so much time wasted, I eventually decided to let the evidence speak for itself.

I decided to never intervene with personal statements, but simply to quote phrases or extracts from documents or public acts, and then write only the strictily necessary for connecting those passages. In other words, I have used the same method that I used to write the book in which I document the swindles and the innumerable crimes perpetrated by many Italian governmental ministers and Italian bureaucrats in order to steal all the treasury funds they themselves nominally allocated for organizing the public service for the protection of the Italian sea and coasts against oil pollution.

At this point, however, it appeared another problem in the shape of a superabundance of evidence.

Drawn by my desire to give a full report of the crimes and prevarications (those, in short, that Colin Crouch more elegantly

15

calls "interactions between elected governments and élites that overwhelmingly represent business interests") intentionally perpetrated to the detriment of the American people and myself by politicians and oil companies, I continually risked going into overdose.

I was afraid I would pile up such a mass of documents and quotations that even the most willing of my courteous readers would feel bewildered.

So that was why I felt I had to back off and remove a part of the enormous amount of material.

And this too was a very long job and in some ways a painful one too, because I sometimes had to delete very significant data.

Thus, after many cancellations, I came to what seemed to me a good point of arrival, so much so that I even tried to get on with the actual book. In short, I went to a graphic designer, a friend of mine, and asked him to layout the manuscript.

But when at last I found myself with the actual book in my hands, I decided that it was not good enough and I began all over again.

So here is the final product.

I just hope I have been able to do what I wanted to do, which is to interest to a number of American citizens, and to make another number of citizens angry.

A small note before I conclude my story.

I realize that, despite my best efforts at offering the documentary evidence, my kind reader will find it hard to believe that Congress and the oilmen really were guilty of the swindles and abuses of power to which I call attention in this book. And above all, that they did this as blatantly as I show here.

In order to help the reader to take on this depressing truth, I recall an ancient Chinese proverb which says "Frogs can jump, not fly". And the fact is that today there are a lot of frogs in the circles we are speaking of here.

Giuseppe Ayroldi

CHAPTER 1

THE OIL POLLUTION PROBLEM

Oil spills and, worst sill, human tragedies are not rare occurrences in the oil business.

On June 1979 Ixtoc 1, the oil exploratory platform situated at around eighty kilometers northwest of the Mexican town of Carmen, in the bay of Campeche, was destroyed by a fire and consequent blast of gas and oil causing an oil spill (about 500,000 oil tons, according to official sources) that was halted only after 295 days. No official report was issued after this disaster, but observers and media reported that a third of the spilled oil burnt, causing enormous atmospheric pollution, while the remaining part spread along the Gulf of Mexico in the form of large floating tar-like slicks that reached almost all the way along the Mexican and Texan coasts.

In March 1980 the Alexander Kielland—built as a drilling rig, but under lease to Phillips Petroleum Company to house offshore workers at the Ekofisk Field in the Norwegian North Sea—capsized, killing 123 of the 212 people on board the "flotel."

Two years later, during preparation for an approaching North Atlantic storm, the Ocean Ranger semisubmersible, drilling the Hibernia field for Mobil Oil of Canada, sank off the coast of Newfoundland; all 84 crew members were lost in the freezing waters.

In July 1988 the Piper Alpha production platform operated

by Occidental Petroleum 120 miles northeast of Aberdeen, Scotland, exploded and sank, killing 167 people, including 2 rescuers.

On March 19, 1989, while the Piper Alpha accident was still under review, a platform operated by ARCO exploded in the South Pass Block 60 off the Louisiana coast. An uncontrolled release of liquid hydrocarbons ignited, destroying the platform and killing seven people. An MMS investigation concluded that poor management of a repair operation was to blame: not only was there an "absence of detailed and coordinated planning for the project," there was a dearth of much-needed "oversight over contractor activities."

In the first decade of this century, the Gulf of Mexico workforce—35,000 people, working on 90 big drilling rigs and 3,500 production platforms—had suffered 1,550 injuries, 60 deaths, and 948 fires and explosions.

This is all history, but the outlook is even blacker. In the future there is the Arctic and its enormous oil reserves.

The Arctic Game

There is a great deal of talk, mostly just lip service, about global warming, the melting of the icecaps and the probable, tragic disappearance of the arctic fox and the polar bear.

Almost nothing, instead, is publicly said about the strategic, political, military and environmental consequences which are sure to follow the opening up of polar routes for navigation and about the race, which had already begun, for the exploitation of the huge food and mining resources present in the Arctic.

As Eni, the public owned Italian oil company, informs us in the March 2013 issue of the *Oil Magazine* entirely devoted to this subject, the Arctic, that is the lands, seas and ices North of the Arctic Circle, latitude 66° N, has large reserves of coal, iron ore, petrol, nickel, cobalt, titanium, bauxite, zinc, copper, gold, silver, platinum and diamonds.

The fish stock of the Arctic (I am still quoting from *Oil Magazine*) includes shrimps, snow crabs, cod, herring, sardines, salmon and trout.

In the petrol sector the Arctic possesses, according to a research carried out by the Norwegian Oil Institute, the Geological Survey of Canada and an international panel of experts,

> "the following, unexplored potential: 82 billion barrels of petrol (12% of the total estimated world deposits), 47 trillion cubic metres of natural gas (30% of the total estimated world deposits), and 44 billion barrels of liquid natural gas (20% of the total estimated world deposits). This comes to the equivalent of a total of approximately 403 billion barrels of petrol (or 20% of the total estimated world deposits), distributed across 60 large deposits."

And the race to exploit all these precious (and, until a short time ago, intact) raw materials has already begun.

In 2012 Arcelor Mittar, the largest steelworks in the world, obtained permission to set in motion a multibillion dollar project for the development of the first iron ore mine on Baffin Island.

In the petrol sector Shell paid more than 2 billion dollars for licences to explore the Alaskan Arctic. Russian shipyards are actively engaged in the construction of petrol rigs suitable for operation in the extreme climatic conditions of the Arctic.

> "The search for petrol and gas in the region is not news, since it has been going on, one way and another, for many decades. Onshore and offshore exploration and exploitation increased enormously in the 1960s, especially in Alaska (Purdhoe Bay, 1967) and in Russia (Tazovskoye, 1962)."

In other words, the "predatory future" exploitation of the Arctic has already started, and nobody is going to call a halt to it or, at least, call for more stringent and effective regulations, even though the dangers involved are enormous.

David Yarnold, President of the National Audubon Society, which monitors the hundreds of thousands of birds which nest in the Alaskan wilderness, says:

"The Arctic exploration efforts carried out by Shell Oil in the past few months are throwing fuel on a fire which is already exploding. According to scientists, so little is known about the methods for coping with petrol spills or similar disasters in freezing water, that the loss of the Deep Water Horizon in the Gulf of Mexico would look like a picnic compared to something of that nature happening in the waters of the Arctic."

In a detailed study commissioned by Lloyd's of London Charles Emmerson, senior researcher in the group of Chatham House experts in London, declared that

"the cleaning up of possible oil spills in the Arctic, especially in areas with ice cover, presents numerous obstacles, which, taken together, form a unique risk which would be difficult to deal with."

and Paul Betts, international economics columnist for the Financial Times, stresses the same thing:

"All the researchers agree that, to date, nobody has any idea how exactly to deal with an oil spill on the polar icecap or on isolated blocks of ice."
(thing this — in my opinion —, almost "automatic", since they do not even know how to deal with an oil spill in the Gulf of Mexico.)

In another study, the accounting and consultancy company Ernst & Young

"lists the high risks and costs of drilling in the Arctic due to the rigid climate, lack of infrastructure, lengthy work schedules and the difficulty of containment and recovery of petrol spills in distant and hostile contexts."

In a programme broadcast by the Deutsche Welle radio, Prof. Marcel Gubaidullin, Director of the Institute for Petrol and Gas at the Federal Northern (Arctic) University of the Russian city of Arkhangelsk, described the reasons that led to the decision to suspend the important Shtokman project in the Barents Sea:

"The Shtokman deposit lies 600 km off the coast of Murmansk. A helicopter cannot reach it even with a full tank. Thus it would be necessary to build a temporary platform in the open sea, or else land on the island of Nowaja Semlja. Furthermore the sea in that area is 340 metres deep. If we placed the Eiffel Tower on the sea bed there, the tip would not even reach the surface. Moreover the sea in that area is very stormy, with waves as high as 27 metres and temperatures which range over the seasons between -55° and +35°C."

"The Russians",

Paul Betts adds,

"still remember the tragedy which took place in 2011, when the floating platform Kolskaya overturned and sank in the Sea of Okhotsk during a terrible storm just after prospecting for Gazprom off the coast of the Kamchatka peninsula. The loss of life (53 people dead or missing) was the heaviest in all the history of accidents in the Russian petroleum sector."

Even more dramatically, we pollute the Arctic even without going there, Yury Morozov, still in *Oil Magazine*, writes:

"Both in winter and in summer the polluted air coming from the areas of Eurasia often blows on this region. From a report by the Arctic Council it shows that the region is constantly threatened by the risk of decomposition due to harmful substances found not only in soil but also in animals.
"For example, in the Arctic zone of Russia, 27 areas have received the nickname "imparked" because here the processes of pollution have caused an evident transformation of the natural geochemical context, as well as serious damage to the atmosphere, degradation of vegetative cover and soil and increase the rate of spread of diseases among the local population. "

Last but not least, the Arctic has sites which the disappearance of the ice will make available for the installation of ballistic missiles, defence and preventive anti-missile systems and other strategic equipment.

The next world war, in short, will be mainly fought in the Arctic.

But let us leave these scenarios, and return to a time a few years ago.

1990: The Congress responds "to the fears and outrage of a nation besieged by oil spills"

On March 24, 1989, as many will remember, the Exxon Valdez oil tanker ran aground on the Captain William Bligh[1] reef and spilled an estimated 11 million gallons of crude oil.

"The catastrophe",

in the Federal Register of Friday, August 30, 1991, the U.S. Coast Guard wrote

"was exacerbated greatly by the unreasonably slow, confused and inadequate response by industry and government, that failed miserably in containing the spill and preventing damage."

and, not being able to continue deceiving a nation which had seen 'live', thanks to the TV, how miserably "industry and government failed to contain the spill and prevent damage" (and, secondly but not less importantly, how false and misleading were their declarations to the American people when they swore that they would be able to contain and remove any oil disaster), the Congress passed the Oil Pollution Act of 1990 (OPA'90) Public Law 101-380 in order

....
1 Captain William Bligh, immortalized in the classic Mutiny on the Bounty, was among the first westerners to sail in Prince William Sound as an officer with Captain James Cook

"to expand prevention and preparedness activities, improve response capabilities, ensure that shippers and oil companies pay the costs of spills that do occur, provide an additional economic incentive to prevent spills through increased penalties and enhanced enforcement, establish an expanded research and development program, and establish a new Oil Spill Liability Trust Fund administered by the U.S. Coast Guard (USCG)."
(Department of Transportation, The Federal Register/ Vol. 59, n. 126/ Friday, July 1, 1994/ Rules and Regulations)

Great: After leaving the oil and shipping industry free to produce, transport, and transform oil products with total disregard for international conventions[2] and national laws, Congress finally decided to make America really safe from oil spills.

And they did it wonderfully! Besides expanding prevention and preparedness activities, improving response capabilities, ensuring that shippers and oil companies pay the costs of spills that do occur and all the other beautiful things that the Department of Transportation has listed on the Federal Register, OPA'90 levels severe obligations on the oil and shipping industry.

For example, Section 4202(a) of the OPA amends CWA section 311(j) formally requires «owners or operators of facilities to prepare and submit to the President of the United States "a plan for responding, to the maximum extent practicable, to a worst case discharge, and to a substantial threat of such a discharge, of oil or a hazardous substance."»

In short, no «owner or operator of facilities» can produce,

....

2 The International Convention for the Prevention of Pollution from Ships, as amended (MARPOL 73/78), London, Feb. 17, 1978; The United Nations Convention on the Law of the Sea (UNCLOS), Montego Bay, Nov. 16, 1964; The International Convention on the Establishment of an International Fund for Compensation for Oil Pollution Damage (Fund 1971), Brussels, December 18, 1971; The International Convention on Oil Pollution Preparedness, Response and Control (OPRC), London, Nov. 30, 1990; The International Convention on Civil Liability for Oil Pollution Damage (CLC 1969), Brussels, Nov. 29, 1969; to cite only a few ones.

transport or transform oil products without having in advance the capacity to clean up the oil disasters they may produce. And the warrantor is the President of the United States!

Fantastic!!

Furthermore, OPA'90 is backed by strict systems of controls and Controllers:

"Under CWA and the Comprehensive Environmental Response, Compensation, and Liability Act (CERCLA), the United States has developed a National Oil and Hazardous Substance Pollution Contingency Plan (NCP) (40 CFR part 300) and has established Area Committees to develop Area Contingency Plans (ACPs) as elements of a comprehensive oil and hazardous substance spill response system."

Wonderful! OPA'90 will absolutely make America safe from oil spills!

The United States, after all, had all the means and the capabilities required in order to keep that promise.

As from 1980, the American Society for Testing and Materials (ASTM)[3] had published the ASTM F 631 – 80 Standard Test Method for full-scale advancing oil spill removal devices[4]. A Standard Test Method, I would like to emphasize, extremely well conceived and proved effective by the International Maritime Organization (IMO), the Agency of the United Nations which deals with oil pollution combat and prevention[5].

....

3   ASTM is the foremost developer and provider of voluntary consensus standards, related technical information, and services having internationally recognized quality and applicability

4   From the book A Century of Progress, Early Standard Development and the Origins of ASTM: «Environmental Protection Agency. EPA, which was formed in 1970, used ASTM standards for electrical generating plants, petroleum tests, and water as a basis for its own standards. Furthermore, industries with interests in environmental protection solicited the assistance of ASTM, leading to the formation of new technical committees such as F-20 on Hazardous Substances and Oil Spill Response and E-35 on Pesticides.»

5   The integral text of the ASTM F 631 – 80 Standard Test Method is photographically reported under Document 1.

In concert with OPA'90, the U.S. David Taylor Model Basin (DTMB) had developed an absolutely excellent test method and mathematical algorithm, based on the Fourier transform[6], to verify under real working conditions (i.e. at sea and with 'real' winds and waves) the performance parameters detected, at ASTM Standards, in a controlled test facility.

In addition, in January 1993 the American Bureau of Shipping (ABS) published a *Guide for Certification of Oil Spill Recovery Equipment* «to provide a framework for the assessment and certification of equipment for oil spill clean-up».

Last but not least, as from the 1970s the Environmental Protection Agency (EPA) was operating a test facility in the Naval Weapons Station ("NWS")-Earle Waterfront, Leonardo, New Jersey: the Oil and Hazardous Materials Simulated Environmental Test Tank (OHMSETT) Research Center in order «to evaluate the performance of equipment designed to detect, monitor, and clean up oil and floating hazardous material spills under environmentally safe conditions» (Summary of U.S. Environmental Protection Agency's Ohmsett testing, 1974 – 1979, Section 1, 'Facility History'). Since, EPA continues, «research and development is that necessary first step in problem solution; it involves defining the problem, measuring its impact, and searching for solutions» (ibidem, foreword).

No less important, ASTM[7] and the U.S David Taylor Model

....

6 The Fourier transform is the mathematical algorithm that decomposes and then recomposes, by means of its inverse formula of synthesis, a complex signal into its constituent frequencies. If the signal is periodic, such as sea waves, the F-transform is a discreet ensemble of values which allow to compare the signals registered in tank test with the signals registered in the open seas, and then to determine, according to ASTM Standard test method, performance parameters of an oil spill removal device when operating in the open seas.

7 (From www.astm.org:) «ASTM International, formerly known as the American Society for Testing and Materials (ASTM), is a globally recognized leader in the development and delivery of international voluntary consensus standards. Today, some 12,000 ASTM standards are used around the world to improve product quality, enhance safety, facilitate market access and trade, and build consumer confidence. ASTM's leadership in international standards development is driven by the contributions of its members: more than 30,000 of the world's top technical

Basin (DTMB)[8] are two well-known institutions enjoying

experts and business professionals representing 135 countries. Working in an open and transparent process and using ASTM's advanced electronic infrastructure, ASTM members deliver the test methods, specifications, guides and practices that support industries and governments worldwide.
[...]
Through 141 technical standards-writing committees, ASTM serves diverse industries ranging from metals to construction, petroleum to consumer products, and many more. When new industries look to advance the growth of cutting-edge technologies, such as nanotechnology and additive manufacturing, many of them come together under the ASTM International umbrella to achieve their standardization goals.
In the arena of global commerce, ASTM International standards are the passports to a successful trading strategy (emphasis supplied). High quality, market-relevant ASTM standards, developed in accordance with the guiding principles of the World Trade Organization, fuel trade by opening new markets and creating new trading partners for enterprises everywhere. From Fortune 500 leaders to emerging startups, ASTM standards help level the playing field so that businesses of all sizes can better compete in the global economy.
[...]
[...]
Beyond its leadership in the area of standards development, ASTM International offers technical training programs for industry and government, as well as proficiency testing, interlaboratory crosscheck programs and newly initiated certification programs, which support manufacturers, users, researchers and laboratories worldwide.
ASTM International world headquarters are located in West Conshohocken, Pa. The Society also has offices in Beijing, China, and Mexico City, Mexico.»

8 (I make copy and paste from the publication: "Historic Mechanical Engineering Landmark David Taylor Model Basin. 1939" edited by The American Society of Mechanical Engineers - 1998): «The David Taylor Model Basin is among the largest of its kind in the world, containing a shallow-water basin, a deep-water basin and a high-speed basin. Using its sophisticated combination of towing carriages, wavemakers, and measuring equipment, engineers are able to determine the seakeeping qualities and propulsion characteristics of ship and craft models up to 40 feet in length. Since it became operational, the facility has provided key support in the development of naval architecture for the Navy, Coast Guard, the Maritime Administration, and maritime industry.» And, in order to make my kind fifteen readers fully aware of the technical capabilities of the David Taylor Model Basin, I continue with copy and paste:
«The DTMB housed at the Naval Surface Warfare Center, Carderock Division (NSWCCD) is state-of-the-art in its construction, conception, and commitment. The DTMB combines five basins in order to make accurate and reliable predictions

worldwide respect.

America, in short, had all the theoretical and practical means necessary to make America really safe from oil pollution.

For its part, the oil industry had established, through a certain MPA (an acronym for the "Marine Preservation Association"), the Marine Spill Response Corporation (MSRC), a non-profit Corporation specifically obliged to «ensure by contract», according to the provisions of OPA'90, «private personnel and equipment necessary to remove[9] to the maximum extent

---

of the performance of ships by research on models.

[…]

To meet requirements for uniformity in the speed of the carriages which tow the models, the rails on the basin walls upon which these carriages will run had to be far straighter and more level than the most perfect railroad track. In fact, to eliminate the effect of gravity on the motion of the towing carriage, the tracks are not straight in the usual sense, but follow the curvature of the earth.

[…]

One notable achievement in early Experimental Model Basin work was the invention of the bulbous bow.

[…]

At DTMB a new set of submarine hull forms was developed. This set of Series 58 hull forms enabled submerged operations at speeds far in excess of those obtainable with more traditional WWII submarines and their predecessors.

[…]

The path to achieving full-scale implementation of highly skewed propellers began in the late 1950s with the development of lifting surface theory at NSWCCD and Massachusetts Institute of Technology.

[…]

Starting in the late 1960s, NSWCCD played leadership role in the development of the basic technology and design methods for the Small Waterplane Twin Hull (SWATH) ship concept.

[…]

Additionally, at NSWCCD, a mathematical scientist named Charles Dawson, developed a revolutionary computational method, called the Dawson Method radically changing and improving the ability of hydrodynamicists to accurately and rapidly perform Kelvin wave system calculations for a ship.

9   "Remove" or "removal" means containment and removal of oil or a hazardous substance from water and shorelines or the taking of other actions as may be necessary to minimize or mitigate damage to the public health or welfare, including, but not limited to, fish, shellfish, wildlife, and public and private property, shorelines, and

practicable a worst-case discharge.»

Perfect! Also because, as it appears from its website (www.msrc.org for the sake of completeness of information hereunder reproduced in full), the MSRC did things big. Very big:

> "A major cornerstone of the U.S. economy is the use of oil and petroleum products to meet the needs of individuals and businesses. In an effort to improve the safety and environmental protection in connection with bringing such products to market, Congress enacted the Oil Pollution Act of 1990 (OPA-90). The Act has numerous provisions, including specific requirements for those engaged in the handling, storage, and transport of oil and petroleum products to "ensure by contract private personnel and equipment necessary to remove to the maximum extent practicable a worst-case discharge."
>
> "The oil and shipping industries acted to provide such capability by supporting the formation of the Marine Preservation Association (MPA) and the Marine Spill Response Corporation (MSRC). MPA, whose membership consists of companies engaged in the business of petroleum exploration and production, refining and marketing, transportation and shipping, provides steady state funding to MSRC in furtherance of the objectives of OPA-90 and the recognition by MPA's Members of the importance of a high quality, dedicated spill response capability.
>
> "MSRC is an independent, non-profit, national spill response company dedicated to rapid response. MSRC's capabilities include a large inventory of vessels, equipment, and trained personnel, complemented by a large contractor workforce in numerous locations in the continental U.S., Hawaii, and the Caribbean. MSRC also provides dedicated access to alternative response technologies such as in situ burn kits and aerial and vessel dispersant spraying.
>
> ### MSRC Today
>
> "Since it was founded in 1990, MSRC has evolved to meet new regulatory requirements and other ever-changing needs. Although MSRC was created to respond to catastrophic spills, today's MSRC has broadened its scope of services. MSRC's mission now

---

beaches (OPA'90, Sec. 1001, 30)

28

includes response to oil spills of any size, shoreline cleanup and, as appropriate, hazardous material spill response and response to spills outside the U.S. (in addition to emergency response services). MSRC can provide additional response capabilities through a network of contractors that make up MSRC's Spill Team Area Responders or STARs. STARs participants are leaders in the environmental cleanup industry. In addition, MSRC recently expanded its mission to include response to non-spill emergencies such as hurricanes, floods, fires, and other disasters. "MSRC continues to grow and change to meet the ever-changing needs of the petroleum and shipping industries and the regulatory communities, whether on a state or federal level. On the U.S. West Coast, Clean Coastal Waters Inc., the Southern California industry funded cooperative has merged with MSRC effective July 1, 2004. The merger with Clean Coastal Waters follows the previous merger with Clean Bay in Northern California effective January 1, 2004. MSRC now offers access to the considerable resources of MSRC, Clean Bay and Clean Coastal Waters operating under MSRC's California Region. Also, in the Pacific Northwest MSRC and Clean Sound Cooperative Inc. merged effective April 1, 2005. The merger combines the personnel and resources of Clean Sound in the Puget Sound area with MSRC's Pacific Northwest resources. It also provides access to MSRC's considerable national resources in the event of a large incident.

Equipment

"One of the most visible hallmarks of MSRC is its broad base of oil spill response resources, at the center of which is a fleet of 15 dedicated Responder Class Oil Spill Response Vessels (OSRVs), designed and built specifically to recover spilled oil. The OSRVs are approximately 210 feet long, have temporary storage for 4,000 barrels of recovered oil, and have the ability to separate oil and water aboard ship using two oil-water separation systems. To enable the OSRV to sustain cleanup operations, recovered oil is transferred into other vessels or barges. In addition to these 15 OSRVs, MSRC also operates two other OSRVs in the San Francisco Bay, CA, four in Southern California, and one in Puget Sound, WA. "MSRC is outfitted with other specialized response vessels and support equipment, including:

- 19 Oil Spill Response Barges with storage capacities between 12,000 and 68,000 bbls
- 8 Shallow Water Barges

- 600,000 feet of boom
- Over 240 skimming systems
- 6 Self-Propelled Skimming Vessels (32 ft. to 58 ft.)
- 7 Mobile Communications Suites comprising telephone and computer connections, and UHF and VHF marine, aviation and business band radios
- Various small crafts and shallow-water vessels
- One C-130 dispersant aircraft
- One King Air dispersant/spotter aircraft"

Impressive, really impressive! Nowhere else in the world can you find (or even imagine) such a «broad base of oil spill response resources» collected all together and immediately available!

Fantastic! Although in this website I do not see anything about the oil spill response capabilities of its 22 OSRVs and its over 240 skimming system so quickly collected by the MSRC.

But it does not matter.

Also because, to judge by the overwhelmingly enthusiastic statements released by politicians and environmentalists all over the U.S., OPA'90 will, once and forever, «improve vessel oil spill response capabilities, and minimize the impact of oil spills on the environment»[10].

In a statement given on February 17, 1993, before the House Subcommittee on Coast Guard and Navigation[11], the Hon. Billy Tauzin, Chairman, said: «This landmark legislation has already played a key role in reducing oil spills in the country and in assuring response capability should a spill occur».

Even more emphatically, the National Resources Defense Council (NRDC), a 'green' Association which was a participant to the Oil Spill Response Negotiated Rulemaking Committee ("Reg. Neg. Committee", the Interagency Coordinating

---

10 DEPARTMENT OF TRANSPORTATION/ Coast Guard/ 33 CFR Part 155/ Discharge Removal Equipment for Vessels carrying Oil/ Interim final rule. Federal Register/ Vol. 58, No 244/ Wednesday, December 22, 1993.

11 House Subcommittee on Coast Guard and Navigation, «Hearing on the implementation of section 4202(a)(6) of the oil pollution act of 1990 requiring oil-carrying vessels to carry discharge response equipment», February 17, March 18, 1993, U.S. Government Printing Office, Washington D.C., 1993.

Committee on Oil Pollution Research established with Title VII, sec. 7001, of OPA'90, see *infra*) and a signatory to the Committee Agreement, issued a 64 pages booklet entitled *Safety at Bay, A Review of Oil Spill Prevention and Cleanup in U.S. Waters*, where it was enthusiastically announced to the American People that the Oil Pollution Act of 1990 is

> "Congress' response to the fears and outrage of a nation besieged by oil spills, most especially the Exxon Valdez disaster in March 1989. The Act was a promise that spill prevention and response would dramatically improve."

just after having, at page 2, rather contradictorily written:

> "Perhaps most importantly, oil spills continue to occur routinely in U.S. waters. Thousands of spills are reported every year, spilling million of gallons of oil. For example, in 1992 the Shoko Maru spilled over 96,000 gallons of crude oil into the Texas City Channel and a leak at an offshore well in Louisiana spilled at least 30,000 gallons before the well caught fire; in 1991 there were 667 spills in the Port of New Orleans, 398 spills in New York Harbor, 239 spills in the Port of Hampton Roads, 235 spills in the Port of Philadelphia, 130 spills in Seattle and 116 spills in Boston Harbor. The amount of oil spilled in these ports alone in one year exceeded 300,000 gallons. Over the past several years, barges alone have accounted for millions of gallons spilled."

and after having also inserted the following "Correction on page 2:"

> "Before this report went to print, our information on a September 1992 spill at an offshore well in Louisiana was that at least 30,000 gallons spilled. However, it was reported in the October 23, 1992 Golob's Oil Pollution Bulletin, published by World Information Systems, that the total amount of crude oil lost from the well in the spill and subsequent fire was 600,000 gallons; of that amount, 106,000 gallons spilled into the water."

At this point, I confess, I am not able to understand how much «Safety at bay» is valid when, as NRDC itself says, after the enactment of OPA'90 «oil spills continue to occur routinely in U.S. waters», over 96,000 gallons of crude oil spilled into the Texas City channel, and 600,000 gallons of crude oil were lost, according the Golob's Oil Pollution Bulletin, in the spill and subsequent fire of an offshore well in Louisiana. And, «over the past several years, barges alone have accounted for millions of gallons spilled.» To say nothing of the «thousands of spills» reported «every year», and which, put together, form a catastrophic oil spill 'diluted', so to say, «every year» along the shorelines and inner waters of the United States, and that almost nobody is aware of.

Anyway, it does not matter: the Oil Pollution Act of 1990 is the "Congress response to the fears and outrage of a nation besieged by oil spills, most especially the Exxon Valdez disaster in March 1989" and it will surely make America absolutely safe against oil spills. The Hon. Billy Tauzin would never lie!

But then: how did it come about that, on April 20, 2010 – that is twenty-one years after the Exxon Valdez oil disaster and about twenty after the enactment of the OPA'90 –, when the Macondo well exploded, both industry and government failed to remove the oil gushing uncontrollably into the Gulf of Mexico?

Or why was it that at points 5 and 6 of the *"Final Report Press Release on the BP Deepwater Horizon disaster"* the Presidentially-appointed "Oil Spill Commission on the BP Deepwater Horizon Disaster" writes that

"Both industry and government were unprepared to contain a deepwater well blowout"

and that

"Companies did not possess the response capabilities they claimed."?

"Elementary, my dear Watson!"

"Elementary, my dear Watson!" Because OPA'90 was

nothing but a cover-up operation intentionally contrived by the Congress of the United States (or, at least, by some colluded sectors of the House Subcommittee on Coast Guard and Navigation) in order to _criminally_ allow the influential élites «engaged in the handling, storage, and transport of oil and petroleum products» keep utilizing the _same_ «specialized response vessels» and the _same_ («specialized»?) oil removal devices that «failed miserably» in the Prince William Sound and in all the catastrophic or non catastrophic oil spills that, following the enactment of the OPA'90, have continued to threaten the marine environment along the coastal areas and the inner waters of the United States.

In short, OPA'90 has _criminally_ allowed MSRC to 'legally' «ensure by contract» **_the most ridiculous and inoperative vessels and oil removal devices ever seen on the face of the Earth_**.

The Hon. Billy Tauzin grows angry? Here are my papers and proof.

Even though the «more than four million barrels of oil» which gushed from the Deepwater Horizon and the 2.2 million gallons of chemicals applied are already more than sufficient proof.

CHAPTER 2

THE NAMEPLATE'S FORMULA
AND OTHER CRIMINAL ACTS

First, a small premise.

After having published the ASTM F 631 – 80 Standard Test Method, ASTM came up with nine other standard methods for testing oil skimmers in a controlled environment and one for testing them in uncontrolled environments.

Total: ten, as we can see from the ASTM document published here under document 1-A.

Now I do not know why ASTM published all these standards, or why on November 2015 they withdrew the ASTM F 631 – 80 Standard Test Method. Much less do I try to figure it out here because I do not want to get into a boring investigation that would certainly push even the most passionate of my courteous readers to regret the money he spent on buying this book.

Therefore, I leave to ASTM the pleasure of explaining to my readers the reason for all these Standards, and here we will only look at the magnificent ASTM F 631 – 80 Standard Test Method, the unique test method that, together with the F808-83(1988) *Guide for Collecting Skimmer Performance Data in Uncontrolled Environments* (withdrawn 1998) was available in 1990.

The ASTM F 631 - 80 Standard Test Method for Full Scale Advancing Spill Removal Devices

The ASTM F 631 – 80 Standard Test Method for Full Scale Advancing Spill Removal Devices (herewith photographically reported in Document 1) consists of 14 Sections and two Appendixes.

Section 1, *"Scope"*, points out the aim of this standard: «The standard provides a method for determining performance parameters of full-scale advancing oil spill removal devices in recovering floating oil when tested in a controlled test facility».

Section 3, *"Summary of Method"*, precisely states where a spill removal device may be tested and what variables will be controlled: «The spill removal device may be tested in a wave/tow tank or other suitable facility with a controllable test environment. Controlled test variables include device velocity relative to water velocity, oil properties and slick thickness, wave conditions, and pertinent device variables.»

«The spill removal device may be tested», I explain for non-engineers, in a extremely wide and long basin[12] endowed with wave generators, oil distribution system, tow mechanism or water flow, in which one can test all existing spill removal devices under the same identical and pre-established test conditions. Under the same identical oil slick thicknesses (one, two or three millimeters, for instance), oil types and properties (viscosity and specific gravity i.e., as light, medium, or heavy), wave characteristics (height, average period or length), and speed of the spill removal devices.

Section 4, *"Significance"*, specifies the *quantitative data* provided by the test method, and the cautions that must be exercised in actual spill situations: «This test method provides quantitative data in the form of oil recovery rates, throughput efficiencies and oil recovery efficiencies under controlled test conditions. The data can be used for evaluating the design characteristic of a particular advancing spill removal device

---

12 OHMSETT, the EPA's test tank, is 20m wide and 200m long.

or as a means of comparing two or more devices (emphasis supplied).

«Caution must be exercised» the extremely serious ASTM warns us, «whenever test data are used to predict performance in actual spill situations, as the uncontrolled environmental conditions which affect performance in the field are rarely identical to conditions in the test tank. Other variables such as mechanical reliability, presence of debris, ease of repair, ease of deployment, required operator training, operator fatigue, seaworthiness, and transportability also affect performance in an actual spill but are not measured with this method. These variables should be considered along with the test data when making comparisons or evaluations of advancing spill removal devices (emphasis supplied).»

Section 5, *"Definitions"*, defines the forms established in Section 4:

Form 1: *Oil Recovery Rate* - the volume of oil recovered by the device per unit of time,

Form 2: *Throughput Efficiency* - the ratio, expressed as a percentage, of the volume of oil recovered to the volume of oil encountered,

Form 3: *Oil Recovery Efficiency* - the ratio, expressed as a percentage, of the volume of oil recovered to the volume of total fluids (oil + water) recovered.

Sections from 6 to 12, then, state in great detail how the tests should be prepared and run and how the test results should be measured and recorded, while Section 13 states precisely how to prepare the test and what entries a table of results should contain for the test run.

Last but not least, Section 14: *"Precision and Accuracy"* and Appendix X2: *"Determination of precision and accuracy"*, outlines how «Statistical measures of accuracy and precision may be determined that will indicate the reliability of test results as well as the degree of standardization in test procedures».

In conclusion, the ASTM F 631-80 Standard Test Method - be it always said as an example - offers anybody the power to determine, *with the utmost certainty and mathematical precision,* the volume of heavy oil that a device can recover per unit of time under different oil slick thicknesses, wave characteristics and device velocities and, hence, the power to compare, <u>under identical and previously established conditions,</u> the capacity of «two or more devices» to recover heavy oil.

In short, it allows us the power to distinguish a «device» that works from one that does not.

But a standard test method that would have that clearly "identified the equipment necessary to remove to the maximum extent practicable a worst case discharge"[13] did not suit oil industry players,

And, all of a sudden, the gracious Coast Guard invented the «Nameplate Formula»

Perplexed Congressmen wondered: "what is this maximum extent practicable that is required by the OPA'90?" And, above all: "how shall we identify the «equipment necessary to remove to the maximum extent practicable a worst case discharge»[14]?

"Experimentally monitoring, measuring and recording, under identical test conditions, the performing capacity of all the existing devices, and then comparing the recorded results", would be the automatic response of any man-in-the-street today, four centuries after Galileo Galilei introduced the experimental method, and two thousand three hundred years after that Archimedes measured the gold contained in the crown of King Gerone of Syracuse by means of an extremely refined series of tests, and Eratosthenes determined the length of the circumference of the Earth by measuring the length of the

....
13 Id. § 1321(j) (5) (c) (iii)

14 Initially the law stated the «best available technology», soon transformed, on request of the oil and shipping industry, into the more flexible and undetermined «best practicable technology», or, even more prudently, into the «best technology economically available».

shadow cast by a pole.

"Experimentally detecting and recording, under the ASTM F 631-80 Standard Test Method, the performance parameters of all the existing vessels and spill removal devices, and then verifying them back in the open seas according to the test method elaborated by the David Taylor Model Basin", any technician would answer, with more precision.

But on Capitol Hill they thought differently.

Instead of saying, as any decent person would have done, that the Oil Recovery Rate of a skimmer is measured in a controlled test facility according to the ASTM F 631-80 Standard Test Method, Congress established (see doc. 2) an *Interagency Committee* charged with establishing "standards and test protocols traceable to national standards to measure the performance of oil pollution perception or mitigation technologies". And, without giving reasons or presenting any technical grounds for this decision, with points 6.2.1, and 6.2.2. of the interim and final proposed rule published in the Federal Register of Friday, August 30, 1991, the Coast Guard proposed the «Nameplate Formula». «To calculate», i.e., the «"Effective" Daily Recovery Capacity for Oil Recovery Devices» by multiplying by 24 the «hourly recovery capacity». What the U.S. Coast Guard, to show they are specifying something different, calls "Throughput rate in barrels"

In essence, we are talking about the meaningless number arbitrarily written by manufacturers on the nameplate of their pretended skimmers.

Or, as an alternative, they talk about «the pump capacity», that is the capacity of the pump attached to the skimmer.

I perfectly understand that no one can really believe that the USCG (I refer to the USCG and not to the Interagency Committee since the ludicrous Nameplate formula has been, at least from a formal point of view, put forward in the Federal Register by the USCG [DOT] - see document 6) really talks such astonishingly idiotic nonsense. Therefore I copy points 6.2.1 and 6.2.2. from the Federal Register already cited - see document 6 or download them directly from the Internet, if you do not believe me (www. federalregister.gov), and see for yourself. And take note also what the USCG, to deceptively insert the verb 'to calculate', pompously call 'The following formula':

> 6.2.1 The following formula shall be used to calculate the effective daily recovery capacity:
> R = T x 24 hours x E where:
> R — Effective daily recovery capacity;
> T — Throughput rate in barrels per hour (nameplate capacity); and
> E — 20 percent efficiency factor (or lower[!] factor as determined by the Regional Administrator).
>
> 6.2.2. For those devices in which the pump limits the throughput of liquid, throughput rate shall be calculated using the pump capacity.

Getting straight to the point, this is what it really boils down to: some blockhead of an oilman or a ship owner takes a little statue of Donald Duck, assembles it on a floater (let's say a log or a couple of empty barrels), puts in his hands an old cast iron pipe and a pump capable of sucking up 1000 barrels of water per hour, sticks a nameplate on it in which is written that it can recover 1000 barrels of oil per hour, the US Government multiplies that figure by 24 and overjoyed says that that Donald Duck is capable of mechanically removing 24.000 barrels of oil per day! Without even considering the sea and weather conditions (temperature, winds, currents, presence, shape and period of the waves), day or night, summer or winter, the type and the thickness of the oily layer, the distance from the coasts, the propagating conditions or the special geographical characteristics of the area where the spill happened.

Fantastic!

I tell you the truth, I never imagined that on the Earth could exist bipeds capable to write nonsense so stupid

However detected, the performance parameters reported on the nameplate or the guarantee of a machine must correspond to the performance parameters which that machine is really able to provide

But there is a point that I must clarify.

Standard test methods can only be used on a «voluntary consensus» basis. No American or non-American law compels manufacturers to follow any (ASTM or other) standard specification or quality definitions. Manufacturers and suppliers are free to produce their machines or their materials as they want, even to their own personal and home-made standards. And their customers are equally free to request that the supplies they require are manufactured and tested in accordance with some specific standards, or else go to the manufacturer who does build and test them according to those specific standards.

However, what is absolutely compulsory under a host of American and non-American laws (anywhere in the world, in short), is that the quantitative data reported on the nameplate or the guarantee of a machine must be <u>real, truthful and verifiable</u>.

If, for instance, the guarantee specifies that the refrigerator in my kitchen has certain technical and performance parameters (e.g. that it reaches 'x' degrees below zero, or that it consume 'x' watts per hour, or even that it is built with a certain type of material), it means, by law, that my refrigerator is <u>really</u> able to reach 'x' degrees below zero, that it really does consume 'x' watts per hour, and that it really is built with that type of material. And this fact, besides making you perfectly aware of what you are going to purchase, also allows you to compare the different refrigerators offered on the market.

And the same holds good for a lamp, for a boiler, for a helicopter, for a tablet, and other type of device or part of a device.

Besides, also the physical characteristics (such as, for instance, mass resistivity, flexural strength, and so on) of all materials must be *experimentally measured*, or, alternatively, mathematically calculated on the basis of physical laws.

Thus the power absorbed by a single-phase AC electric motor can be either measured directly with a power meter, or, alternatively, calculated by multiplying the input current (measured with an ammeter) by the applied voltage (measured with a voltmeter) and the cosine of the phase shift φ. In the same way, the deformation in the middle F of a classic simple or fixed reinforced concrete beam placed under the stress of a distributed load is calculated under the theory and formulas applied in the science of construction with the formula $E = 5PL^3/384EI$, where P is the load, L the length of the beam, E the module of elasticity (determined by an ultrasonic test or a dynamic test in the laboratory) and I the momentum of inertia.

Besides - a slight digression -, would you ever buy a washing machine only because the Hon. Billy Tauzin said that «this is a landmark washing machine»?

Moreover, also the mathematical laws of Physics themselves are either based on data experimentally collected or validated by controlled experiments.

Kepler formulated the laws of the motion of the planets around the Sun on the basis of both the data experimentally collected by Tycho Brahe and the geometry of the conics invented two hundred years B.C. by Apollonius of Perge. In the same way the speed of falling bodies in a vacuum has been determined, denying Aristotle, by Galileo Galilei measuring the rate of fall of a sphere of bronze down an inclined plane (or, they say, throwing, a artillery ball and a musket ball from the top of the Tower of Pisa).

«I greatly doubt» Galileo writes in the *Discorsi e Dimostrazioni Matematiche Sopra Due Nuove Scienze* [Discourses and Mathematical Demonstrations on two New Sciences] «that Aristotle *ever experienced* how true it is that two stones, one ten times greater than the other, let fall at the same time from a height, say a hundred arms, were so different in their speed, which on arrival of the greater on the ground, the other was not have even fallen ten arms»[15].

....

15 In 1971 the experiment was repeated on the moon. When he was on the surface

And, in 1820, the Danish Doctor Hans Christian Oersted showed that a magnet is deflected by an electric field by placing a current-carrying wire near a compass. Likewise, led by a sure instinct (as Einstein said) Amedeo Avogadro, Alessandro Volta, André Marie Ampère, Michael Faraday, James Prescott Joule, James Clerk Maxwell and other respected scientists completed the magnificent book of Classic Physics by demonstrating their ideas with controlled experiments, or putting hand to the partial derivatives.

And even when, thanks mainly to the study of the electric charges, radioactivity and electromagnetic radiation in its various forms, a host of new scientists at the turn of the nineteenth century designed a universe beyond the confines of classical physics, Galileo and the experimental method was the beacon that guided all their steps.

Thus Max Plank found that the energy is emitted not continuously but in discrete, tiny packages which would come to be called "quanta" by studying the spatial distribution of the radiation of a black body cavity, and Sir J.J. Thomson came to the discovery of the electron by studying the behavior of the electric charge in rarefied gases. Moreover, and in spite of its imposing mathematical and 'humanistic' proofs, Einstein's Theory of General Relativity was shown to be accurate only after its hypotheses had been validated by measuring the angle variation between two stars in the presence of a solar eclipse, the gravitational red shift of light, and the precession in the perihelion of Mercury's orbit.

In the same way, in elementary particles physics new ideas and new hypotheses - as, for example, the existence of quarks or

---

of the moon, Astronaut David R. Scott, commander of the mission Apollo 15, dropped together an hammer and a feather, and, as shown by the registration made for the American television, both the objects touched the ground at the same time. «Galileo was right!», said Scott at the end of the experiment.

The "experiment", indeed, was effected not to prove that Galileo was right (as is evidenced by the fact that the equation $s = -\frac{1}{2}gt^2$ that measures the distance travelled by an initially stationary object falling for time t, such as all Galilean equations, does not contain the mass), but to make a tribute to Galileo and to the experimental method.

Higgs boson—are studied (or validated) in enormous laboratories and by means of enormous machines as storage rings (invented by Professor Bruno Touschek), or in the centers for the study of the cosmic rays.

Likewise the experimental method is crucial in the pharmaceutical industry, where new medicines are tested according to lengthy and very severe protocols before being put on the market. Even sport scores are measured by the race stewards with the meter and the stopwatch in accordance with a series of precise and well established rules which may also be called standard specifications. And when they cannot be measured, as in boxing or soccer, the score often gives rise to debates and disputes.

Even when you buy a pair of new shoes (or go to a jumble sale and get a good, second-hand pair), you first try them and maybe even ask with what material they were manufactured.

Furthermore, if, in the absence of any standard specification, I take a pool five or six square meters wide, fill it with ten or twenty centimeters of water and half a meter of oil, and test my oil removal device in it (this is no flight of the imagination: Donald Duck apart, here in Italy the prime supplier of [supposed] oil skimmers to the Italian Ministry of the Environment, the OCS of Padua, has, centimeter more or centimeter less, done exactly that), surely also that Donald Duck would be able to recover 50 or 100 (or even more) cubic meters of oil per hour.

The Congress of the United States - this, I regret to say, is the proven truth that emerges from the facts - has enacted a law that, besides being terribly stupid, _intentionally_ lacks any actual quantitative data which «can be used for evaluating design characteristics of a particular advancing spill removal device or as a means of comparing two or more devices». For evaluating, in short, whether a device is able to clean up an oil spill or not.

The Book of Genesis and the resistance to Standards

I am well aware that my kind fourteen American readers

might have a hard time psychologically in believing what I have just written.

So to really make clear the paramount importance of standard specifications and testing procedures in the words of recognized experts, I download from the Internet just a few lines from the book *A Century of Progress, Early Standard Development and the Origins of ASTM* (www.astm.org), and all your psychological difficulties, or inability to believe, will immediately disappear:

"One of the first materials specifications is found in the Book of Genesis: "Make thee an ark of gopher wood; rooms shalt thou make in the ark, and shalt pitch it within and without with pitch." Prior to the 19th century industrial revolution, craftsmen told their suppliers in similarly basic language what kinds of materials they desired. Shipwrights preparing to build a sturdy vessel usually ordered live oak, the toughest hardwood available in Europe and North America, rather than softer white oak, because they knew from experience that live oak was more durable. Craft experience was indeed key because artisans had no instruments to measure the tensile strength, chemical composition, and other characteristics of a given material.

"The industrial revolution opened a new chapter in the history of material specifications. Locomotive builders, steel rail producers, and steam engine builders who used revolutionary new materials such as Bessemer steel could no longer rely on craft experiences of centuries past. The new materials and techniques invented during this period required new technical expertise. Moreover, manufacturers encountered numerous quality problems in end products such as steel rails because suppliers furnished inferior materials. American rails were so poorly-made, in fact, that many railroad companies preferred British imports, which were more expensive but reliable.

"To avoid such problems, some manufacturers issued detailed descriptions of material to ensure that their supplies met certain quality standards. For example, when a federal arsenal ordered gun steel from a steel mill, the contract included several pages of specifications detailing chemical composition and physical characteristics.

"The federal government also asked the steel makers to take

a sample from each steel batch which was then subjected to a few simple tests determining its tensile strength and elasticity. To perform quality checks, American steel companies used new testing equipment such as the Riehle steel tester or a version of Tinius Olsen's Little Giant, which were used to determine tensile strength."

In short: since the times of Genesis, that is to say, from the dawn of recorded time, «craftsman told their suppliers what kinds of materials they desired.»

And, we must recognize that the U.S. Coast Guard also told their suppliers what kind of oil removal devices they required. Or, in the language of the post industrial revolution, they have stipulated exact standard requirements.

Let's see, hence, how the USCG and the then President of the MSRC Rear Admiral John D. Costello implemented and what standard requirements (in short: the Nameplate Formula) they themselves stipulated.

The Coast Guard «clarifies» and Rear Admiral John D. Costello, the President of MSRC, «strongly supports»: **«The requirements set forth in the rule are for planning purposes only and are not intended as performance standards.»**

In the "additional information" — herewith photographically reported in Document 7-A — sent on January 27, 1992, to the "Executive Secretary, Marine Safety Council, (G-LRA-2/3406), (CGD 91-034/CGD 90-068), U.S. Coast Guard Headquarters, 2100 Second Street, S.W., Washington D.C. 20593-0001", Rear Admiral John D. Costello, the President of MSRC and a member of the Oil Spill Response Negotiated Rulemaking Committee (Reg. Neg. Committee) "takes the opportunity" to provide the following "MSRC SUPPLEMENTAL COMMENTS ON VESSEL RESPONSE PLAN ISSUES":

"I. «DEFINING RESPONSE TO THE "MAXIMUM EXTENT

PRACTICABLE" AND ADVERSE WEATHER»"
"MSRC is in the process of implementing plans to substantially increase oil spill response capability in United States coastal, tidal and certain other waters. MSRC's plans were developed based on a 30,000-ton spill scenario in the offshore environment. To identify the specific equipment and other capability, MSRC used the Delphi method, assembling expert consultants to develop and apply planning assumptions—a method not unlike what the Coast Guard is now undertaking to implement the regulations for vessel response plan requirements of the Oil Pollution Act of 1990 (OPA 90). MSRC believes that these planning efforts relate directly to the issues raised by the Coast Guard in its efforts to define "maximum extent practicable" response.

"OPA 90 requires that vessels have response plans that ensure by contract or other approved means the capability to respond to a worst case discharge to the "maximum extent practicable." See OPA 90 § 4202. In essence, this requirement establishes the level of private response capability that the owner or operator of a vessel must have available and be able to manage to continue to transport oil.

"In its various papers addressing the definition of the term "maximum extent practicable," the Coast Guard has proposed to objectively define this term through various planning factors to arrive at an acceptable quantity, quality and location of equipment, personnel and other resources. We believe this approach is appropriate, and should satisfy Congress' intent in OPA 90 to require credible planning and the private resources for respond to large-scale spills and also provide an objective means for vessels owners and operators to evaluate response contractors' capabilities to meet owner and contractor response obligations.

"A. Use "planning assumptions" - not "performance standards"

"MSRC necessarily had to use various "planning assumptions" to develop the quantity and type of response equipment for its plans. The Coast Guard likewise is examining various planning factors. As stated in its paper on the definition of maximum extent practicable, **any standards and measurements established must be viewed strictly as planning standards, not performance standards**." (emphasis supplied.)

"MSRC agrees that performance standards, in the emergency response setting of an oil spill, are unwise, unworkable and misleading, because they create unrealistic expectations for future spills. Any one planning factor can vary substantially in any given spill, because of factors beyond the control of the response organization, including, but not limited to, the characteristics of the oil, changing weather, location of the spill, oceanographic conditions, time of occurrence, condition of the damaged vessel, presence of debris, and regulatory requirements, to name but a few. Any individual factor may vary, but reasonable midpoint assumptions for each factor may produce a reasonable equipment inventory with an appropriate mix of response tools. In an actual spill event, those assets can only be applied to that particular spill using a reasonable best effort considering all the circumstances. "Individual planning assumptions therefore should not be given greater weight than they deserve. In fact, they should not be called "standards" at all—only assumptions and factors used to develop and justify the level of capability required (emphasis supplied). That capability specification should consist of three elements: (1) an equipment system requirement; (2) a location requirement for that equipment; and (3) a mobilization requirement.""

Not satisfied with this, in a letter - herewith photographically reported under Document 8 - sent on July 30, 1992 to the same "Executive Secretary, Marine Safety Council" the gallant and unnaturally intelligent Rear Admiral stresses again that

"The Vessel Response Plan Rule Should Not Establish Performance Standards"
"This section clarifies that the purpose of the proposed regulations is to affect planning for oil spill response. MSRC strongly supports the Coast Guard's clarification in the preamble and in the language of the proposed rule that "the requirements set forth in the rule are for planning purposes only and are not intended as performance standards." 57 Fed. Reg. at 27,516. Planning factors include a host of stated and unstated assumptions. Each planning factor can vary substantially in any given spill, because the factors represent a gross simplification of complex elements, many of which are beyond the control of response organizations. Although any individual factor may vary in an actual spill,

appropriate assumptions for each factor, together with sound professional judgment, can produce an equipment inventory with a reasonable mix of response tools. In an actual spill event, those assets can only be applied to that particular spill using a reasonable best effort considering all the circumstances."

and, referring to point b. of SECTION 155.1020 – DEFINITIONS of the proposed rule, our gallant Rear Admiral points out that **«The definition of "contract or other approved means" should be clarified to avoid implication of performance standards»**:

"The proposed rule rightly reflects the Reg Neg Agreement that **the vessel response plan rules are not intended to establish spill clean up performance standards** (emphasis supplied). However, as currently proposed, the definition of "contract or other approved means" does not clearly reflects this intent. The definition specifies that the equipment and personnel must be available "within stipulated response times in specified geographic areas." 57 Fed. Reg. at 27,538 (proposed rule). The Coast Guard should clarify that this is meant to be directed to the <u>capability</u> of meeting the response times under a standard set of assumptions, and not interpreted to require that the response resources must meet the specified response times as performance standards."

Clear, absolutely clear: no standards at all. Not even that one about arriving at the scene of the disaster "within stipulated response times in specified geographic areas. 57 Fed. Reg. at 27,538."

According to the unimaginably intelligent Rear Admiral John D. Costello – excuse me if I linger to annotate such clear prose – the planning of 'something' (of a wall, of a medicine, of a therapy, or even an oil contingency plan) can be made based on assumptions that have no connection with reality. According to the unimaginably intelligent Rear Admiral John D. Costello Napoleon at Austerlitz ordered his artillery over the assumed range of his guns and not on the actual and mathematically and experimentally ascertained range of his gunfire.

In short, according to Coast Guard and the unimaginably intelligent Rear Admiral John D. Costello oil contingency plans can be designed based on "assumptions" that have nothing to do with the actual functional-technical and operational capacities of the skimmers and the vessels involved.

And on this point I might as well stop. The Coast Guard and the unimaginably clever Rear Admiral John D. Costello have already perfectly explained *why* MSRC and the U.S. Government *failed miserably in containing and removing* <u>any</u> oil spills which occurred along the coasts and the inner waters of the United States.

And this is not all!

Rear Admiral John D. Costello is in fact at pains to explain *how* he has identified MSRC's specific equipment and other capabilities, and the operational program he used to collect them. And all I have to do here is carry on with the copy and paste procedure.

Rear Admiral John D. Costello explains how he identified "MSRC's specific equipment and other capabilities"

In the second of the above quoted letters Rear Admiral John D. Costello took care (perhaps in order to be able to point to the Coast Guard as the guilty party, if necessary) to explain 'how' he identified the specific equipment and other MSRC's capabilities:

> "To identify the specific equipment and other capability, MSRC used the Delphi method, assembling expert consultants to develop and apply planning assumptions—a method not unlike what the Coast Guard is now undertaking to implement the regulations for vessel response plan requirements of the Oil Pollution Act of 1990 (OPA 90)"

Extraordinary!
But: what is the «Delphi method» actually?
He kindly enough explained it, with a flood of caveats such as:

"INFORMATION PROVIDED HEREIN INVOLVES ASSUMPTIONS MADE SOLELY FOR PLANNING PURPOSES AND DOES NOT REFLECT PREDICTED ACTUAL PERFORMANCE IN ANY PARTICULAR SPILL EVENT. NOTHING IN THIS INFORMATION IS INTENDED OR SHOULD BE INTERPRETED AS A PROMISE OR STANDARD OF PERFORMANCE"

the Rear Admiral himself from the cover of "Appendix I, MSRC Supplementary Comments, Pollution Response Equipment, Skimmer Capability and Limits", here reported under Document 7-B:

"MSRC's equipment inventory was developed through a multi-phased process. In addition to applying in-house experience and knowledge, MSRC used the Delphi approach, incorporating the advice and recommendations from many knowledgeable sources including the oil industry, ITOPF, Aleyeska, OSSC in Southampton, NOFI, USCG, MMS, cooperatives and contractors"

I.e. «after the «advice» of the *same* consultants, the *same* oil companies and the *same* manufacturers of the *same* (so-called) skimmers and oil recovery vessels which «failed miserably» in Alaska in 1989 and which from 1989 to the present, have continued to fail during the «thousands of spill» which «continue to occur routinely in U.S. waters».

And there is more!

In "Appendix IV, MSRC Supplementary Comments, Response Time and Skimming assumption", in fact, Mr. John D. Costello does not hesitate to state from exactly what exceptional information source he «calculated removal capacities» of his extraordinary «equipment inventory»:

"MSRC used the data provided by Robert Schulze in his World Catalog of Oil Spill Response Products"

I.e. the data published on a catalog which, as Mr. Schulze

51

himself honestly warns us, publishes whatever information the manufacturers send him.

And, as is apparent from the data reported in the table (published here under "Document 7-B"): *Marine Spill Response Corporation, Major Pollution Response Equipment List*, the «Effective daily recovery capacities» are amazing. Or rather, *hyper amazing*.

The equipment inventory collected by MSRC with the Delphi method can work with fantastic «MFR's Name Plate capacities», under any kind of operating environment, all types of oil and with sea conditions up to 6!

Yes! It just keeps on getting better! America has been rendered absolutely safe against the risk of oil spills!

But, one naïve but spontaneous query comes to mind: how come this assembly of hyper powerful equipment failed to remove the oil spilled from the Macondo well?

Here is the answer for my kind readers (and for the U.S. Coast Guard).

The operational program

As I have shown above (I summarize in deference to my courteous readers), to collect *those same* skimmers and *those same* vessels which «failed miserably» in the Prince William Sound in 1989 and which between 1989 and the present «failed miserably» to remove the Macondo well oil spill and the «thousands of spills» which «continue to occur routinely in U.S. waters», Rear Admiral John D. Costello followed an operational program consisting of five steps, namely:

Step 1: Rear Admiral John D. Costello and the U.S. Coast Guard transform the "performance standards" into "planning assumptions", and then they say that the "planning assumptions" are not in any way challenging;

Step 2: The U.S. Coast Guard states that the "Effective daily recovery capacity for oil removal devices" is "calculated" multiplying by 24 the (senseless) number arbitrarily written by manufacturers on the nameplate of their devices;

Step 3: Skimmers manufacturers arbitrarily write a (senseless) number on the nameplates of their devices, and send that number to Mr. Schulze;

Step 4: Mr. Schulze publishes that number in his "World Catalog of Oil Spill Response Products";

Step 5: Rear Admiral John D. Costello, the U.S. Coast Guard and the Government of the United States multiply that number by 24 and say: "Oh what marvelous oil skimmers!!"

CONCLUSION:

"Historically, recovery from major spills has amounted to only a few percent, if there was any recovery at all."
(Congressional Research Service, Office of Technology Assessment, *Coping with an Oiled Sea*, 1990.)

CHAPTER 3

NEWS FROM THE MEDIA

I think it is useful and perhaps even instructive to see how the media reported the colossal failure of the (alleged) "operation clean up" arranged in 2010 by BP in the Gulf of Mexico, and what politicians and oilmen told to the American people.

Here are the reports from a number of newspapers:

Top Executives and an unidentified "group of oil industry engineers" explain why MSRC didn't even try to recover the oil spilled in the Gulf of Mexico

James Mckinley Jr. and Leslie Kaufman write on the *International Herald Tribune* of May 12, 2010:

> "The heart of the industry's plan to contain the oil falls to Marine Spill Recovery, a nonprofit corporation formed in 1990. It is maintained largely by fees from the oil companies. Judith Roos, a vice president of the group, said «most of its equipment was bought in 1990. "The technology has not changed that much since then," she said.»

> "Allison Nyholm, a police adviser with the American Petroleum Institute, the main industry lobby, said that blowout scenarios

were rare and needed handling on case-by-case basis."

"One of the best tools is how you bring the best professionals together to respond to the spill, she said"

(confusing, perhaps, «the best professionals» with the little magician from the Lord of the Rings).

"What is Plan B[16]?" The answer, oil industry engineers are acknowledging, was to deploy technology that has not changed much in 20 years.

[...]

"Once oil was flowing into the water, the methods of dealing with it have changed little in decades, environmentalists say."

Fantastic! Apart from having kindly confirmed

a) That OPA'90 did not «expand prevention and preparedness activities, improve response capabilities», as the Department of Transportation in a deliberate lie wrote in the Federal Register, and

b) that the «broad base of oil spill response resources» which failed miserably in the Gulf of Mexico in 2010 was the same «broad base of oil spill response resources» that «failed miserably» in the Prince William Sound in 1989 – just as I have shown all through this book,

the good Ms. Judith Roos and an anonymous *group of oil engineers* (perhaps too ashamed to put their names to such a stupid statement) stress that MSRC failed to clean up the oil gushed from the Macondo well because «most of its equipment was bought in 1990».

....

16 It emerges, from the web and the International Herald Tribune of May 2.2010, that no Plan B existed, but only five suggestions offered by five experts, which go (a) from *Stop outsourcing* offered by John Hofmeister, former president of Shell and author of *Why We Hate the Oil Companies: Straight Talk from an Energy Insider*, to (b) *Forget acoustic sensors*, offered by Ken Arnold, energy industry consultant, to (c) *Avoid dispersants*, offered by Riki Ott, marine toxicologist and author of *Not One Drop: Betrayal and Courage in the Wake of the Exxon Valdez Oil Spill*, to (d) *Soak up the oil*, offered by Terry Hazen, microbial ecologist at Lawrence Berkeley National Laboratory, to (e) the advice *Do nothing* offered by Kevin M. Yaeger, assistant professor of marine sciences at the University of Southern Mississippi. In short, oil industry had no Plan A, no Plan B, but only a Plan C-Corexit.

Actually, I am struggling to follow this reasoning. In fact, I just can't.

Even the ancient Egyptians and Babylonian scribes knew that if a noria, or a mill, worked yesterday, they would work again today, tomorrow and the day after that. In the same way, the cochlea and the hydrostatic balance, invented by Archimedes in the III Century B.C., are still used today in industry and science – just like the sunshade, the loom for weaving by hand, the ladder and the steelyard.

In short, if an oil removal device worked in 1990 with the extraordinary oil recovery rates reported in the table *Marine Spill Response Corporation, Major Pollution Response Equipment List* (herewith reported, I remember, in Document 7-B), it would have worked with the same oil recovery rates in 2010 and would still work even in the year 3972.

Likewise, if something doesn't work, it won't work today, tomorrow or the day after tomorrow. Thus it was that, being stupid, the «broad base of oil spill response resources» «bought in 1990» by Rear Admiral John D. Costello with the Delphi method "failed miserably" either in 1989 in Alaska or in 2010 in the Gulf of Mexico. And Rear Admiral John D. Costello, who said that they were able to recover oil spills at the extraordinary oil recovery rates reported in the table *Marine Spill Response Corporation, Major Pollution Response Equipment List*, is a public criminal today just as he was yesterday and will remain so tomorrow.

Also because, as they used to say in Southern Italy, *if one is born a sparrow, one cannot die an eagle.*

"It was in any case stupid to expect that MSRC had the capacity to capture the volume of oil gushing from the Gulf well", *stressed Steve Benz, MSRC president and former BP executive*

The on-line edition of June 29, 2010 of the Washington Post

reports:

> "Should the Industry's capacity have been greater than it is? That's a fair question," said Steve Benz, MSRC president and former BP executive. He stressed that the U.S. Coast Guard set benchmarks for how much equipment and manpower large oil-recovery companies should have. Also, he said, any standing operation would have difficulty immediately capturing the volume of oil gushing from the Gulf well.
> "If this happened again, should we already have in place 20,000 people and 1000 boats?" Benz asked. "You can't built a firehouse that big and have it make any reasonable economic sense. You need to prevent the fire in first place."

Silly ruminations aside, Mr. Steve Benz, MSRC president and former BP executive and therefore in the know, kindly confirms that

- When the NRDC said that «Safety is at bay»;
- When the Department of Transportation assured the American citizens that OPA'90 will «reduce the risk of oil spills, improve vessel oil spill response capability and minimize the impact of oil spills on the environment»;
- When Hon. Billy Tauzin said that «This landmark legislation has already played a key role in reducing oil spills in the country and in assuring response capability should a spill occur»;
- When the National Resources Defense Concil enthusiastically announced to the American People that the Oil Pollution Act of 1990 was "a promise that spill prevention and response would dramatically improve."
- When BP asserted that «the combined response could skim, suck up or otherwise remove 20 million gallons of oil each day from the water»;
- When oilmen stressed that «MSRC was created to respond to catastrophic oil spills»;
- When MSRC assured that it had the capacity «to remove to the maximum extent practicable a worst-case discharge»;
- When MSRC proclaimed it was able to work under any kind

58

of operating conditions and all types of oil with the fantastic «MFR's Name Plate capacities» listed in the table "Marine Spill Response Corporation, Major Pollution Response Equipment List" herewith published under Document 7-B, ***they made a false declaration to the American people***. So says of Mr. Steve Benz, MSRC president and former BP executive.

Delinquents and imbeciles.

But let's go on and see, for the sake of having all the information, what else Associated Press journalists Justin Pritchard, Tamara Lush and Holbrok Mohr, contributed by Ted Bridis and Eileen Sullivan in Washington, Brian Skoloff in Grand Isle, La., Harry R. Weber in Houston, and Jason Bronis in New Orleans tell us about the «embarrassing aspects» in BP's response plan. Even if many of these aspects are already known to the American public, since they have been widely reported in blogs and newspapers[17].

> "Glaring errors and omissions in BP's oil spill response plans have exposed a slapdash effort to follow environmental rules, outraging Gulf Coast residents who can see on their beaches how unprepared the company was.
> [...]
> "BP PLC's 582-page regional spill plan for the Gulf, and its 52-page, site-specific plan for the Deepwater Horizon (www.americanscientist.org) rig, vastly understate the dangers posed by an uncontrolled leak and vastly overstate the company's preparedness to deal with one. The lengthy plans were approved by the federal government last year before BP drilled its ill-fated well.

And, considering the reliability of the source, I continue to quote:

> "In its Deepwater Horizon plan, the British oil giant stated: "BP

---

17 For example: BP Response Plans Severely Flawed/Fox News; (www.foxnews.com)

Exploration and Production Inc. has the capability to respond, to the maximum extent practicable, to a worst case discharge, or a substantial threat of such a discharge, resulting from the activities proposed in our Exploration Plan."

[...]

"The plans contain wildly false assumptions about oil spills. BP's proposed method to calculate spill volume judging by the darkness of the oil sheen is way off. The internationally accepted formula would produce estimates 100 times higher.

[...]

"Look," Louisiana Gov. Bobby Jindal said, "it's obvious to everybody in south Louisiana that they didn't have a plan, they didn't have an adequate plan to deal with this spill".

[...]

"In responses to lengthy lists of questions from AP, the Interior Department, which oversees the MMS, appears to concede there were problems with the two oil spill response plans: «Many of the questions you raise are exactly those questions that will be examined and answered by the presidential commission as well as other investigations into BP's oil spill,»" said Kendra Barkoff, spokeswoman for Interior Secretary Ken Salazar. She added that Salazar has undertaken reforms of MMS[18].

[...]

"BP asserts that the combined response could skim, suck up or otherwise remove 20 million gallons of oil each day from the water. But that is about how much has leaked in the past six weeks—and the slick now covers about 3,300 square miles, according to Hans Graber, director of the University of Miami's satellite sensing facility. Only a small fraction of the spill has been successfully skimmed[19]. Plus, an undetermined portion has sunk

----

18 The Mineral Management Service (MMS) is the Agency formed in 1982 by Reagan's Interior Secretary James Watt in support of his goal to open unprecedented reaches of U.S. territorial waters to oil and gas exploration. On June 2010 the agency name was changed from MMS to Bureau of Ocean Energy Management, Regulation and Enforcement (BOEMRE).

19 The verb "skimmed" is wrong: this «small fraction of the spill» hasn't been «successfully skimmed», but it has been almost entirely absorbed with oil absorbing booms. And in fact, according to Christian Science Monitor (www.csmonitor.com), 2.000 miles or 50.000 tons of lightly soiled absorbing booms vainly used in the Gulf to corral the gushing oils have been burned.

to the bottom of the Gulf or is suspended somewhere in between."

...and so forth till «glaring error» n. 47. Or, may be, n. 46.5 – sorry to be fussy –, since the last report: «BP asserts that the combined response could skim, suck up or otherwise remove 20 million gallons of oil each day from the water» is, both, true and false at the same time.

It is true, in fact, because that figure: «20 million gallons of oil each day», is just the sum of the oil recovery capacities reported, according to the formula established by the Coast Guard (i.e. legally), by manufacturers on the nameplates of MSRC's «broad base of oil spill response resources».

But it is false too, because, as Professor Hans Graber observed and we ourselves have seen directly or on the TV, the spilled oil has not been "removed", but has simply been sunk and transferred to the sea floor by spraying immense quantities of chemicals with airplanes.

However, since as the Greeks (always the marvelous Greeks!) taught us two thousand and five hundred years ago, nothing can be true and false at the same time, it is absolutely certain that this number: «20 million gallons of oil each day», cannot be true and false at the same time. And, since the «more than four million barrels of oil gushed into the Gulf» were measured by scientists and, even more convincingly, the TV images were surely true (let me believe my own eyes!), it is sure and mathematically proved that the oil recovery capacities stamped, according to the rule established by the U.S. Coast Guard (i.e. legally), on the nameplates of the stupid equipment inventory assembled by Rear Admiral John D. Costello are untrue to say the least.

In other words, to put it bluntly, the Nameplate Formula is a criminal, Machiavellian operator criminally passed by the Congress of the United States to criminally permit the companies «engaged in the handling, storage, and transport of oil and petroleum products» to continue using the same (so-called) machines which "failed miserably" in Alaska whilecriminally giving the American people the false idea that America had

61

been made absolutely safe from the threat of oil pollution. To *criminally* allow, in short, the oil industry to (legally) falsely assert in front to the American people that they can «skim, suck up or otherwise remove 20 million gallons of oil each day from the water.»

Besides: what Rear Admiral John D. Costello repeatedly and in capital letters did say to the Executive Secretary, Marine Safety Council? «INFORMATION PROVIDED HEREIN INVOLVES ASSUMPTIONS MADE SOLELY FOR PLANNING PURPOSES AND DOES NOT REFLECT PREDICTED ACTUAL PERFORMANCE IN ANY PARTICULAR SPILL EVENT. NOTHING IN THIS INFORMATION IS INTENDED OR SHOULD BE INTERPRETED AS A PROMISE OR STANDARD OF PERFORMANCE».

...And the betrayal continues

Not knowing what else to invent to make Americans believe that he was deeply concerned with the oil pollution that was ravaging the Gulf of Mexico, President Barack Obama appointed a specific Oil Spill Commission

> «an independent, nonpartisan entity, directed to provide a thorough analysis and impartial judgment. The President charged the Commission to determine the causes of the disaster».

Well, this report is now posted on www. oilspillcommission.gov but, in spite of reading it carefully, I have found no reference whatsoever to the responsibilities of the U.S. Coast Guard for the approval of the criminal «nameplate formula».

I cannot, of course, copy here all this report in order to demonstrate this affirmation of mine. I am sure, anyway, that at least a number of my more patient readers will take the trouble go to the above reported website, and verify for themselves whether or not I have told the truth here.

Nevertheless, for those who do not wish to waste time on governmental websites, I will use copy and paste from the more relevant sections which refer to the Oil Pollution Act of 1990 and to the Marine Spill Response Corporation.

But this is a matter for the following chapter.

CHAPTER 4

THE REPORT TO THE PRESIDENT

After having with heartfelt participation premised that

"The explosion that tore through the Deepwater Horizon drilling rig last April 20, as the rig's crew completed drilling the exploratory Macondo well deep under the waters of the Gulf of Mexico, began a human, economic, and environmental disaster.
"Eleven crew members died, and others were seriously injured, as fire engulfed and ultimately destroyed the rig. And, although the nation would not know the full scope of the disaster for weeks, the first of more than four million barrels of oil began gushing uncontrolled into the Gulf—threatening livelihoods, precious habitats, and even a unique way of life. A treasured American landscape, already battered and degraded from years of mismanagement, faced yet another blow as the oil spread and washed ashore. [...] The costs from this one industrial accident are not yet fully counted, but it is already clear that the impacts on the region's natural systems and people were enormous, and that economic losses total tens of billions of dollars."
(Report to the President, Foreword, page VI)

the National Commissioners address the core question:

"On May 22, 2010, President Barack Obama announced the creation of the National Commission on the BP Deepwater Horizon Oil

Spill and Offshore Drilling: an independent, nonpartisan entity, directed to provide a thorough analysis and impartial judgment. The President charged the Commission to determine the causes of the disaster, and to improve the country's ability to respond to spills, and to recommend reforms to make offshore energy production safer. And the President said we were to follow the facts wherever they led.

"This report is the result of an intense six-month effort to fulfill the President's charge."

(Ibidem, same page)

Fantastic! Here they are really in earnest!

However, I perceive small problems when, in paragraph "complex systems almost always fail in complex ways", they add that:

"As the Board that investigated the loss of the Columbia space shuttle noted, "complex systems almost always fail in complex ways." Though it is tempting to single out one crucial misstep or point the finger at one bad actor as the cause of the Deepwater Horizon explosion, any such explanation provides a dangerously incomplete picture of what happened—encouraging the very kind of complacency that led to the accident in the first place. Consistent with the President's request, this report takes an expansive view."

(Ibidem, page VIII)

When, namely, «consistent with the President's request», in a couple of lines the National Commissioners transform the President's charge «to determine *the causes of the disaster*» into «*the cause of the Deepwater Horizon explosion*». When, in other words, in a couple of lines the National Commissioners reduce the far larger and more important request from the President «to determine *the causes* [plural] *of the disaster* [a term that certainly includes the *oil* disaster]» into the by far smaller and limitative «*cause* [singular] *of the Deepwater Horizon explosion* [a term that certainly *excludes* the oil disaster]».

In short: there is nothing about the «nameplate formula», nothing about the «Delphi method», nothing about the

66

reasons why, after having failed miserably in containing and removing the oil gushed in the Alaskan seas in 1989, industry and government once again failed miserably in containing and removing the oil spill in the Gulf of Mexico in 2010, nothing about the «more than four million barrels of oil gushed uncontrolled into the Gulf—threatening livelihoods, precious habitats, and even a unique way of life», nothing about the «treasured American landscape, already battered and degraded from years of mismanagement,» which «faced yet another blow as the oil spread and washed ashore».

Furthermore, and with all respect for the National Commissioners and their «expansive view», their chic quotation: «As the Board that investigated the loss of the Columbia space shuttle noted, "complex systems *almost always* fail in complex ways"»[20] is wrong twice over.

First because, with all the respect for «the Board that investigated the loss of the Columbia space shuttle», any assertion is true only after you have demonstrated that it is true and in line with the facts, and this has been so since the time of Aristotle and Chrysippus of Soli. Even those assertions—be it said with the maximum respect—made by «the Board that investigated the loss of the Columbia space shuttle».

Second, because, as I read in Wikipedia, the Columbia Accident Investigation Board (CAIB) (i.e. what the National Commissioners call «the Board that investigated the loss of the Columbia space shuttle», http://caib.nasa.gov/) confirmed that the loss of Columbia was a result of damage sustained when, approximately 82 seconds after launch from Kennedy Space Center's LC-39-A, a piece of foam insulation the size of a small briefcase broke off from the Space Shuttle external tank (the 'ET' main propellant tank) under the aerodynamic forces of launch. The debris struck the leading edge of the left wing, damaging the Shuttle's thermal protection system (TPS) which shields the vehicle from the intense heat generated by atmospheric

----

20 I.e.: "complex systems not always fail in complex ways"

compression during re-entry. So, when, at about 8:58:20 a.m. EST, February 1, 2003, the Orbiter re-entered the atmosphere, the damaged area allowed hot gases to penetrate and destroy the internal wing structure, rapidly causing the in-flight breakup of the vehicle.

In short, the loss of Columbia was caused by a small piece of foam broken off from the Space Shuttle external tank. I.e. by one single crucial misstep.

Moreover, as the Physicist and Nobel laureate Richard Feynman proved with a simple public test, the Space Shuttle Challenger disaster—lift off on a cold morning, at 11:38:00 a.m. EST on January 28, 1986—was also caused by a failure of O rings which sealed the joint between the two lower segments of the Shuttle's right solid rocket booster.

In short—sorry for the National Commissioners and their 'expansive' point of view—, also the Space Shuttle Challenger disaster was caused by a single crucial misstep.

(Very different and 'expansive', instead, is the question of human responsibilities for those disasters. But this is not the matter of this book.)

By the by: what bad actor would the Commission have ever found, when the bad actors were seated in the Commission? What bad actor could Commission's Co-Chair William K. Reilly find, when in the years 1989 to 1993 he was the Administrator of the Environmental Protection Agency (EPA), the regulating agency which happily approved the ludicrous «nameplate formula» crime in 1990? Or Commission's Member Frances G. Beinecke, President of the Natural Resources Defense Council (NRDC), the «non-profit corporation» that, in 1990[21], happily did the same thing? Only the Commander of the USCG and the Hon. Billy Tauzin are missing, and the team would have been complete!

In a sense, and be it said with the maximum respect, the National Commissioners (and President Obama behind them)

....
21 In 1990 the NRDC was a member of the Oil Spill Response Negotiated Rulemaking Committee.

behaved like the Baron of Munchausen, who pulled himself out of the swamp by pulling his own hair.

Anyway, gentle and *always general* blame for government regulations are seldom found either in the Report or in the attached papers.

In the paragraph «Key Commission Findings» of the paper: "Oil Spill Commission Landmark Report on Gulf Disaster Proposes Urgent Reform of Industry and Government Practices to Overhaul U.S. Offshore Drilling Safety/ Definitive Investigation Finds Gulf Disaster was Preventable; Similar Future Disasters Likely Without Action by Congress, Administration, and Industry/ *Growing U.S. Dependence on Domestic Offshore Oil Makes Reform a National Priority; Independent Government Safety Agency and Industry Safety Institute Both Needed*" released on January 11, 2011 11:00 a.m. EST, for instance, the National Commissioners write that:

> "*Government regulation was ineffective*, and failed to keep pace with technology advancements in offshore drilling." (emphasis supplied)

and, at points 5 and 6 of the same paragraph:

> (Point 5): "Both industry and government were unprepared to contain a deepwater well blowout. [...] At the time of the Macondo well blowout on April 20, 2010, the federal government was unprepared to oversee a deepwater well-containment effort."

> (Point 6): "Both industry and government were unprepared to respond to a massive deepwater oil spill, even though such a spill was foreseeable. [...] Companies did not possess the response capabilities they claimed. [...] Since the Exxon Valdez oil spill in 1989, neither industry nor the government has made significant investments in spill-response research and development, so the clean-up technology used following the Deepwater Horizon spill was largely unchanged."

The National Commissioners—this is the point—generically say that «government regulation was ineffective,» that «both industry and government were unprepared to respond to a massive deepwater oil spill,» that «Companies did not possess the response capabilities they claimed», but they do not say _why_ government and industry were unprepared, or _why_ companies did not possess the response capabilities they claimed, and far less do they say where and at what point «government regulation was ineffective».

Besides, in a paper ten pages long, would it really have been so difficult or irrelevant to write that "«companies did not possess the response capabilities they claimed» because the criminal «nameplate formula» allowed them to _falsely claim_ oil response capabilities they did not possess"?

But, if the National Commissioners say nothing about the causative «nameplate formula» crime, they very accurately point out _how_ oilmen usually conduct their business.

And I continue with copy and paste.

"When I first started working, they didn't care whether they killed you or not!" _remembered one offshore veteran._ "In other words, 'we are going to get it done, regardless.'

"During the 1960s", in the paragraph «Pushing Technological Frontiers—and Physical Limits» the National Commissioners point out,

> "the sheer technological challenges and the necessity to complete work as quickly as possible compromised safety. Project profitability depended on how soon production could be brought online. Drilling vessels were contracted on day-rates, increasing time pressures. Production processes were highly interdependent: delay in one place could cause delays elsewhere. So there were relentless demands to drill the wells, install the platforms, and get the oil and gas flowing. "When I first started working, they didn't care whether they killed you or not!" remembered one offshore veteran. "In other words, 'we are going to get it done,

regardless.' There was no suing like people are suing now. Back then, if you got hurt, they just pushed you to the side and put somebody else in.

"Accident rates for mobile drilling vessels remained unacceptably high, especially for jackups. Blowouts, helicopter crashes, diving accidents, and routine injuries on platforms were all too common. Facilities engineering on production platforms was a novel concept. Platforms often had equipment squeezed or slapped together on the deck with little concern or foresight for worker safety. Crew quarters, for example, could sometimes be found dangerously close to a compressor building.

"Federal oversight followed the philosophy of "minimum regulation, maximum cooperation." Between 1958 and 1960, the U.S. Geological Survey Conservation Division, the regulatory agency then overseeing offshore drilling, issued outer continental shelf Orders 2 through 5, requiring procedures for drilling, plugging, and abandoning wells; determining well productivity; and the installation of subsurface safety devices, or "storm chokes." But the Offshore Operators Committee (representing leaseholders) persuaded regulators to dilute Order 5 to permit waivers on requirements for storm chokes. **Significantly, the orders neither specified design criteria or detailed technical standards, nor did they impose any test requirements. Companies had to have certain equipment, but they did not have to test it to see if it worked.**" (emphasis supplied)

(E.g.: **"Companies had to have certain oil spill removal equipment, but they did not have to test it to see if it worked**.")

"In general, as a 1973 National Science Foundation study concluded, «**the closeness of government and industry and the commonality of their objectives have worked against development of a system of strict accountability.**» (emphasis supplied.)

"Lax enforcement contributed to the lack of accountability. The U.S. Geological Survey freely granted waivers from complying with orders and did not inspect installations regularly. Federal and state regulatory bodies were underfunded and understaffed. In 1969, the Gulf region's lease management office had only 12 people overseeing more than 1,500 platforms. Even those trained

inspectors and supervisors often lacked experience in the oil business and a grasp of its changing technological capabilities. "Each oil well has its own personality, is completely different than the next, and has its own problems," observed one consultant in 1970. "It takes good experienced personnel to understand the situation and to cope with it." Too often on drilling structures, he complained, one found inexperienced supervisors; employees who overlooked rules and regulations (the purpose of which they did not understand); and, perhaps most troubling, even orders from bosses to cut corners—all of which created conditions for an "explosive situation."
(Report to the President, pages 26 and 27)

Oil Companies, in short, have always done what they liked. And the political leaders both within the Executive Branch and Congress have always done what the oil companies wanted.

Oil companies wanted neither specified design criteria nor detailed technical standards, and, «Significantly, the orders neither specified design criteria or detailed technical standards, nor did they impose any test requirements.»

Oil companies did not want Order 5, and the Offshore Operators Committee (representing leaseholders) persuaded regulators to dilute Order 5 to permit waivers on requirements for storm chokes.

Oil companies wanted «Lax enforcement on accountability», and «The U.S. Geological Survey freely granted waivers from complying with orders and did not inspect installations regularly.»

Oil companies want to use «the same blunt response technologies—booms, dispersants, and skimmers—that were used in Alaska to limited effect,» and the U.S. Coast Guard produced the Nameplate Formula.

... And there is worse, much worse.

«The political leaders within both the Executive Branch and Congress and the Chief Executive and Commander-in-

Chief have failed to ensure that agency regulators have had the political autonomy needed to overcome the powerful commercial interests that have opposed more stringent safety regulation.»

After having pretty well declared, on page IX of their Report, that

"it is impossible to argue that the industry or the country were prepared for a disaster of the magnitude of the Deepwater Horizon oil spill. Twenty years after the Exxon Valdez spill in Alaska, the same blunt response technologies—booms, dispersants, and skimmers—were used, to limited effect. On-the-ground shortcomings in the joint public-private response to an overwhelming spill like that resulting from the blowout of the Macondo well are now evident, and demand public and private investment. So do the weaknesses in local, state, and federal coordination revealed by the emergency. Both government and industry failed to anticipate and prevent this catastrophe, and failed again to be prepared to respond to it."

in the paragraph: "Impediments to Safety Regulation" the National Commissioners address the core question:

"The federal government has never lacked the sweeping authority required to control whether, when, and how valuable oil and gas resources located on the outer continental shelf are leased, explored, or developed. As described at the outset, the government's authority is virtually without limitation, traceable to both its authority as proprietor and as sovereign, then further bolstered by the President's inherent authority as Chief Executive and Commander-in-Chief to ensure the security of the nation. **The root problem has instead been that political leaders within both the Executive Branch and Congress have failed to ensure that agency regulators have had the resources necessary to exercise that authority, including personnel and technical expertise, and, no less important, the political autonomy needed to overcome the powerful commercial interests that have opposed more stringent safety regulation."** (emphasis supplied.)

(Report to the President, page 67)

But why - the question arises spontaneously, as an old Italian columnist used to say - did political leaders within both the Executive Branch and Congress fail to ensure that agency regulators had the resources necessary to exercise that authority, including personnel and technical expertise, and, no less important, the political autonomy needed to overcome the powerful commercial interests that fought against more stringent safety regulation?

«Elementary, my dear Watson!»

"Revenue generation - enjoyed both by industry and government - became the dominant objective. But there was a hidden price to be paid for those increased revenues. Any revenue increases dependent on moving drilling further offshore and into much deeper waters came with a corresponding increase in the safety and environmental risks of such drilling. Those increased risks, however, were not matched by greater, more sophisticated regulatory oversight. **Industry regularly and intensely resisted such oversight, and neither Congress nor any of a series of presidential administrations mustered the political support necessary to overcome that opposition. Nor, despite their assurances to the contrary, did the oil and gas industry take the initiative to match its massive investments in oil and gas development and production with comparable investments in drilling safety and oil-spill containment technology and contingency response planning in case of an accident."**

(Report to the President, page 56) (emphasis supplied)

and

"MMS became an agency systematically lacking the resources, technical training, or experience in petroleum engineering that is absolutely critical to ensuring that offshore drilling is being conducted in a safe and responsible manner."

(Ibidem, page 57)

...and the scapegoat on which lay the blame in case of an

accident.

It is hardly surprising "therefore" if

"the technology

("American" technology)

"available for cleaning up oil spills has improved only incrementally since 1990. Federal research and development programs in this area are underfunded: In fact, Congress has never appropriated even half the full amount authorized by the Oil Pollution Act of 1990 for oil spill research and development. In addition, the major oil companies have committed minimal resources to in-house research and development related to spill response technology. Oil spill removal organizations are underfunded in general and dedicate few if any resources to research and development. Though some commentators and industry representatives have argued that more research and development would not have allowed for a more effective spill response because no technology will ever collect more than a fraction of spilled oil, the fact is that neither industry nor government has made significant investments in improving the menu of response options or significantly improved their effectiveness. Thus any argument about the limited potential of response technology is speculative."

(Report to the President, page 269)

Clear, perfectly clear. As is the fact that Oilmen have forked tongues like snakes.

In fact, when they write their contingency plans, they declare that they "could skim, suck up or otherwise remove 20 million gallons of oil per day", and when they have to justify their failures, or privately discuss their work with regulators, they argue that "no technology will ever collect more than a fraction of spilled oils."

And, to top it off, these are the reasons why President Obama «left open the possibility of expanding offshore leasing beyond the Gulf of Mexico and Alaska»:

"In 2008, President George W. Bush and Congress ended the

leasing moratoriums on vast stretches of the U.S. outer continental shelf, and Bush proposed opening new areas for exploration. In a March 31, 2010 announcement, President Barack Obama scaled back Bush's plan, but he left open the possibility of expanding offshore leasing beyond the Gulf of Mexico and Alaska. **The President defended his position by observing, «oil rigs today generally don't cause spills.»"** (emphasis supplied)
(The White House, Office of the Press Secretary, Remarks by the President in a Discussion on Jobs and the Economy in Charlotte, North Carolina, April 2, 2010, http://www. whitehouse.gov. – Report to the President, page 53)

Because, in short **"oil rigs today generally don't cause spills"**." And on April 20 (i.e. not even 18 days afterwards: maybe Obama brings bad luck too?) the Deepwater Horizon exploded.

«The legislative promise»

The 1978 Outer Continental Shelf Lands Act Amendments, the National Commissioners honestly remind us in the paragraph entitled «The legislative promise»,

> "promised full consideration of concerns for environmental protection. The Act provides that "[m]anagement of the outer Continental Shelf shall be conducted in a manner which considers economic, social, and environmental values of the renewable and nonrenewable resources contained in the outer Continental Shelf, and the potential impact of oil and gas exploration on other resource values of the outer Continental Shelf and the marine, coastal, and human environments." It further requires that the timing and location of exploration, development, and production of oil and gas take environmental factors into consideration, including: existing ecological characteristics; an equitable sharing of development benefits and environmental risks among the regions; the relative environmental sensitivity and marine productivity of areas; and relevant environmental and predictive

information. Based on an evaluation of these and other factors, the Act directs the Secretary of the Interior to select the "timing and location of leasing, to the maximum extent practicable, so as to obtain a proper balance between the potential for environmental damage, the potential for the discovery of oil and gas, and the potential for adverse impact on the coastal zone.

"A host of other laws, many enacted by Congress during the 1970s surge of environmental legislation, buttress these promised priorities. Of particular relevance to oil and gas leasing on the outer continental shelf is the National Environmental Policy Act requirement that federal agencies prepare environmental impact statements for all major federal actions significantly affecting the human environment. Those detailed statements must include not only discussion of the immediate adverse impacts on the natural environment that might result from the federal action, but also the "socio-economic" effects of those impacts. The Magnuson-Stevens Fishery Conservation and Management Act requires agencies to analyze the potentially adverse impacts of oil and gas activities on fish habitat and populations, and provide conservation measures to mitigate those impacts. The Endangered Species Act requires federal agencies to determine the potential adverse impact of oil and gas activities on endangered and threatened species, limits activities that harm individual members of such species, and bars altogether activities that place such species in jeopardy. The Marine Mammal Protection Act imposes limits on activities that injure or even harass marine mammals. The National Marine Sanctuaries Act requires consultations to guard against harm to marine sanctuary resources from oil and gas leasing activities. The federal Clean Water Act imposes permitting requirements on any discharge of pollutants into navigable waters from such activities. And, the Oil Pollution Act of 1990, supplemented by a Presidential Executive Order, imposes a panoply of oil-spill planning, preparedness and response requirements on fixed and floating facilities engaged in oil and gas exploration, development, and production on the outer continental shelf."

Fantastic! Really fantastic!! Congress has really made America absolutely sure against the risk of oil spills!

At this point, however, "somebody" (the Hon. Billy Tauzin, for example) ought to kindly explain to my readers how it is that, o despite the 1978 Outer Continental Shelf Lands Act Amendments and its "promised full consideration of the concerns for environmental protection",

o despite OPA'90 and despite the enormous lot of "other laws" enacted by Congress during the 1970s in a surge of environmental legislation,

"oil spills continued to occur routinely in U.S. waters", and a "treasured American landscape, already battered and degraded from years of mismanagement, faced yet another blow".

This is what it all boils down to: the Outer Continental Shelf Lands Act Amendments, the OPA'90 and the whole panoply of oil-spill planning, preparedness and response requirements are nothing but a swindle of the most Machiavellian and sordid kind, carefully set up by Congress in order to allow the oilmen to carry on doing exactly as they please without any regulation or control while persuading the American people that America has been rendered really safe from oil spill damage.

And the dangerousness of these Machiavellans dramatically increase if one looks at them in the context of the terrible risks linked with the drilling and the exploitation of oil fields.

☹ ☹ ☹

I'm sorry to have to use a rather difficult engineering language in the following paragraphs. However, to give my readers (who in 98% of cases certainly are neither an engineer nor a geologist) at least the certainty that I am not telling lies, nor exaggerating a little out of righteous indignation, I keep copy and pasting from the "Report to the President."
Beginning from the paragraph:

«The Inherently Uncertain Cementing Process»

"Cementing an oil well is an inherently uncertain process.
"To establish isolation across a hydrocarbon zone at the bottom of

a well, engineers must send a slug of cement down the inside of the well. They then pump mud in after it to push the cement down until it "turns the corner" at the bottom of the well and flows up into the annular space. If done properly, the slug of cement will create a long and continuous seal around the production casing, and will fill the shoe track[22] in the bottom of the final casing string. But things can go wrong even under optimal conditions. If the cement is pumped too far or not far enough, it may not isolate the hydrocarbon zones. If oil-based drilling mud contaminates the water-based cement as the cement flows down the well, the cement can set slowly or not at all. And, as previously noted, the cement can "channel," filling the annulus unevenly and allowing hydrocarbons to bypass cement in the annular space. Given the variety of things that can go wrong with a cement job, it is hardly surprising that a 2007 MMS study identified cementing problems as one of the "most significant factors" leading to blowouts between 1992 and 2006.

"Even following best practices, a cement crew can never be certain how a cement job at the bottom of the well is proceeding as it is pumped. Cement does its work literally miles away from the rig floor, and the crew has no direct way to see where it is, whether it is contaminated, or whether it has sealed off the well."

(Report to the President, page 99)

And the challenges grow frighteningly when – as the National Commission correctly stresses in the paragraph: "The Challenges of Deepwater Drilling at the Macondo Well." of Chapter 4: "But, who cares, it's done, end of story, [we] will *probably* be fine and we'll get a good cement job" – we move from theory to reality.

And I carry on copy and pasting:

"High Pressures and Risk of a Well Blowout"

"Oil forms deep beneath the Earth's surface when organic materials deposited in ancient sediments slowly transform in response to

---

22 The hole drilled in the formation below the pay sands.

intense heat and pressure. Over the course of millions of years, these materials "cook" into liquid and gaseous hydrocarbons. The transformed materials can flow through porous mineral layers, and tend to migrate upward because they are lighter than other fluids in the pore spaces. If there is a path that leads to the surface, the hydrocarbons will emerge above ground in a seep or tar pit. If an impermeable layer instead blocks the way, the hydrocarbons can collect in porous rock beneath the impermeable layer. The business of drilling for oil consists of finding and tapping these "pay zones" of porous hydrocarbon-filled rock.

"The weight of the rocks above a pay zone can generate tremendous pressure on the hydrocarbons. Typically, the deeper the well, the higher the pressure—and the higher the pressure, the greater the challenges in safely tapping those hydrocarbons. The first oil wells were drilled on land and involved relatively low-pressure oil reservoirs. As oil companies drilled farther offshore, they encountered large hydrocarbon deposits, often in more porous and permeable geologic formations, and, like at the Macondo well, at ever-higher pressures.

"The principal challenge in deepwater drilling is to drill a path to the hydrocarbon-filled pay zone in a manner that simultaneously controls these enormous pressures and avoids fracturing the geologic formation in which the reservoir is found. It is a delicate balance. The drillers must balance the reservoir pressure (pore pressure) pushing hydrocarbons into the well with counter-pressure from inside the wellbore. If too much counter-pressure is used, the formation can be fractured. But if too little counter-pressure is used, the result can be an uncontrolled intrusion of hydrocarbons into the well, and a discharge from the well itself as the oil and gas rush up and out of the well. An uncontrolled discharge is known as a blowout."

And, the better to highlight this point, I also copy the annotations reported by the National Commissioners:

"Pore Pressure and Fracture Gradient"

"Pore pressure is the pressure exerted by fluids in the pore space of rock. If drillers do not balance pore pressure with pressure from drilling fluids, hydrocarbons can flow into the wellbore (the hole drilled by the rig, including the casing) and unprotected sections of the well can collapse. The pore pressure gradient, expressed as an equivalent mud weight, is a curve that shows the increase of pore pressure in a well by depth.

"Fracture pressure is the pressure at which the geologic formation is not strong enough to withstand the pressure of the drilling fluids in a well and hence will fracture. When fracture occurs, drilling fluids flow out of the wellbore into the formation instead of circulating back to the surface. This causes what is known as "lost returns" or "lost circulation." The fracture gradient, expressed as an equivalent mud weight, is a curve that shows the fracture pressure of rocks in a well by depth."

and:

"Drilling Terminology"

"Drilling through the seafloor does not differ fundamentally from drilling on land. The crews on any drilling rig use rotary drill bits that they lubricate and cool with drilling mud—an ordinary name for what is today a sophisticated blend of synthetic fluids, polymers, and weighting agents that often costs over $100 per barrel. The rig crews pump the mud down through a drill pipe that connects with and turns the bit. The mud flows out holes in the bit and then circulates back to the rig through the space between the drill pipe and the sides of the well (the annulus), carrying to the surface bits of rock called cuttings that the drill bit has removed from the bottom of the well. When the mud returns to the rig at the surface, the cuttings are sieved out and the mud is sent back down the drill string. The mud thus travels in a closed loop.

"As the well deepens, the crew lines its walls with a series of steel tubes called casing. The casing creates a foundation for continued drilling by reinforcing upper portions of the hole as drilling progresses. After installing a casing string, the crews drill farther, sending each successive string of casing down through the prior ones, so the well's diameter becomes progressively smaller as it gets deeper. A completed deepwater well typically telescopes down from a starting casing diameter of three feet or more at the wellhead to a diameter of 10 inches or less at the bottom." (Report to the President, pages 90 and 91)

...And the risks do not end here.

"Drill Pipe, Mud, Casing, Cement, and Well Control"

"Those drilling in deepwater, just like those drilling on land, use drill pipe, casing, mud, and cement in a series of carefully calibrated steps to control pressure while drilling thousands of feet below the seafloor to reach the pay zone. Drilling mud, which is used to lubricate and cool the drill bit during drilling, plays a critical role in controlling the hydrocarbon pressure in a well. The weight of the column of mud in a well exerts pressure that counterbalances the pressure in the hydrocarbon formation. If the mud weight is too low, fluids such as oil and gas can enter the well, causing what is known as a "kick." But if the mud weight is too high, it can fracture the surrounding rock, potentially leading to "lost returns"—leakage of the mud into the formation. The rig crew therefore monitors and adjusts the weight (density) of the drilling mud as the well is being drilled—one of many sensitive, technical tasks requiring special equipment and the interpretation of data from difficult drilling environments."
(Ibidem, same page.)

But let's complete the story. Let us try to understand why the Macondo well exploded, and why eleven workers died.

CHAPTER 5

"THE COST OF SUCH A DEPARTURE FROM THE STANDARDS OF EXCELLENCE" AND "THE CULTURE OF REVENUE MAXIMIZATION"

The Deepwater Horizon exploded, explains Ugo Bilardo, Professor Emeritus of Production and Transport of Oil and Gas at the University 'La Sapienza' in Rome, because BP's engineers did not take into account that the oil in the Macondo prospect was very light and rich in gases like all the wells in the area, and the sediments themselves, full of gas pockets, clearly showed. Thus they erroneously assembled a blow out preventer (BOP) designed for heavy oils on the wellhead.

At the paragraph: "Prior Blowout Preventers Failure" of the Article: *Five thousand Feet and Below: The Failure to Adequately Regulate Deepwater Oil Production Technology*, Mark A. Latham, Professor of Law at Vermont Law School, writes that

> "When one considers the reliability questions that MMS, engineers, and others in the industry raised concerning blowout preventers over the years, it is shocking that this technology serves as the final failsafe mechanism to control well pressure in an emergency. As a starting point in considering the questionable reliability of blowout preventer technology, we must realize that the Deepwater Horizon spill was not some unexpected, unanticipated, rare occurrence. It was an entirely foreseeable

event. That is, the Deepwater Horizon was not the first time that a blowout preventer failed to stop a catastrophic flow of oil after pressure control was lost at a well in the Gulf of Mexico.

"In 1979, the Mexican national oil company PEMEX, while conducting oil exploration activities at the Ixtoc I well, experienced pressure control problems. Realizing the critical need to capture well control, the Ixtoc I operators activated the shear rams on the blowout preventer. But once activated, the rams failed to shear through the pipe and stem the flow of oil. Thus, one lesson from the Ixtoc I spill was that, when most needed, blowout preventers can utterly fail.

"More recently, in 2009, there was a well blowout off the coast of Australia. The Montara spill raged for more than ten weeks before flow was stopped.

"Although this well was only in 250 feet of water, it further demonstrates the technical difficulties associated with capping a well even in relatively shallow waters."

And then again, at the paragraph: "MMS Research into and Knowledge of Unreliable Blowout Preventers"

"In 2004, MMS retained WEST Engineering Services "to answer the question 'Can a rig's blowout preventer (BOP) equipment shear the pipe to be used in a given drilling program at the most demanding condition to be expected, and at what pressure?'"

"This was not simply a question of engineering curiosity, since "[t]he well control function of last resort is to shear pipe and secure the well with the sealing shear ram. As a result, failure to shear when executing this final option would be expected to result in a major safety and/or environmental event.

"The 2004 WEST Engineering study pointed to improvements in drill pipe strength, coupled with the need to use larger, heavier pipe in deepwater drilling, which together "adversely affect[] the ability of a given ram BOP to successfully shear and seal the pipe in use." This concern was more than a theoretical possibility because "WEST is currently aware of several failures to shear when conducting shear tests using the drill pipe that was to be used in the well.

Others had also raised concerns about the reliability of blowout preventers. In a paper presented at the 2003 Offshore Technology Conference, the authors noted that "[f]loating drilling rig downtime due to poor BOP reliability is a common and very costly issue confronting all offshore drilling contractors.

Blowout preventer unreliability has not escaped scrutiny in the Deepwater Horizon congressional investigations. One congressional committee's investigation noted that "in numerous cases, blowout preventers have failed to operate, often with catastrophic consequences. The blowout preventer installed on the Macondo well failed to control the blowout."

(Mark A. Latham, *Five thousand Feet and below: The Failure to Adequately regulate Deepwater Oil Production Technology*, 38 B.C. Envtl. Aff. Rev. 343 (2011), http.//lawdigitalcommons. bc.edu/ealr/vol38/iss2/7)

According to one congressional committee's investigation, "errors in cementing the well" caused the explosion, and the Deepwater Horizon exploded because "the blowout preventer installed on the Macondo well failed to control the blowout."

But,

"Industry contended that blowout-preventer stacks — the critical last line of defense in maintaining control over a well — were more reliable than the regulations recognized, warranting less frequent pressure testing, MMS conceded and halved the mandated frequency of tests."

(Report to the President, page 73)

Wow!!

The National Commission on the other hand speaks of errors (perhaps a question of centralizers) in cementing the well that severely compromised the primary cement job.

The media reported a "skirmish" on the rig between a BP well site leader and crew members employed by Transocean, the rig's owner, on the morning of the blast. Representative Nick J. Rahal II, Democrat of West Virginia and chairman of the House Committee on Natural Resources—it emerges from the *International Herald Tribune* of May, 28, 2010—said that the morning of the accident BP let workers from Schlumberger leave the rig without conducting a special test on the quality of the cement work. Almost all media reported that BP had a delay of 43 days, and was desperately trying to recover time and costs.

BP, for its part, shifted (or tried to shift) the entire blame onto Transocean's and Halliburton, who in their turn shifted it back to BP.

Of course, I don't know why BP used the riskier (or wrong) method of casing, or why they assembled a wrong BOP on top the wellhead. Or why they let workers from Schlumberger leave the rig without conducting the special test on the quality of the cement work.

The trouble is that not even Obama knew why!

Mr. Obama and the «political leaders within both the Executive Branch and Congress» did not know anything about the lunatic Nameplate Formula;

Mr. Obama and the «political leaders within both the Executive Branch and Congress failed to ensure that agency regulators had the political autonomy needed to overcome the powerful commercial interests that opposed more stringent safety regulations»;

Mr. Obama and the «political leaders within both the Executive Branch and Congress» have never seen what happened daily (or almost daily) along the coasts and the inner waters of the United States. All they did when the Macondo well exploded, was to come out with statements that are «full of sound and fury, signifying nothing».

Mr. Obama and the «political leaders within both the Executive Branch and Congress» never knew about the «failures» and the «budgetary restraints» that the National Commissioners report in the paragraph entitled

«Overlaps and "underlaps."»:

"The lack of resources extended beyond MMS. The United States Coast Guard is responsible for regulating the "safety of life and property on Outer Continental Shelf (OCS) facilities, vessels, and other units engaged in OCS activities." Because most drilling rigs and even some production platforms fall under the definition of "vessels," part of the responsibility for regulating their safe operation (and full authority for certifying their seaworthiness) is within the jurisdiction of the Coast Guard. But just when the need for Coast Guard oversight increased during the 1990s—as industry drilled in deeper waters farther offshore and used more ambitious floating drilling and production systems—it, too, faced more severe budgetary restraints. Accordingly, the Coast Guard failed to update its marine-safety rules—the last major revision was in 1982—to reflect the industry's new technology. The resource plight worsened further following the terrorist attacks of September 11, 2001, given the nation's overriding need to focus on border and port security. The Coast Guard's "solution"—to transfer much of its responsibility for fixed platform safety to MMS in 2002—eerily echoed earlier cycles of expanding MMS's mandate in the face of inadequate resources, stretching its capabilities thinner still. The practical effect of the Coast Guard and MMS's shared responsibility for offshore safety has been the presence of "overlaps" in jurisdiction that have required the renegotiation of informal interagency agreements ever since 1989—the continuance of which has left MMS with "underlaps" in resources."

Or what the National Commissioners write in the paragraph entitled:

«The Culture of Revenue Maximization»:

"When Interior Secretary Watt moved regulatory oversight of offshore energy exploration and production to a new entity that was also responsible for collecting revenue from the activity it regulated, he created a new agency that inexorably came to be dominated by its focus on maximizing that revenue.
"For at least the past 15 years, every former MMS Director has freely acknowledged that the royalty issues have taken most of the Director's time—at the expense of offshore regulatory oversight. In 1995, as the United States faced global competition for oil exploration and development capital during a period of

low prices, Congress enacted the Deep Water Royalty Relief Act. It provided a suspension of royalty payments on a portion of new production from deepwater operations.

"But when prices and volumes increased, the sheer amount of money at stake—literally billions of dollars (MMS total onshore and offshore revenues for 2008 were $23 billion)—compelled even greater attention, as the White House, members of Congress, and certainly the states each advanced competing notions of how those sums might best be spent. Litigation, new regulations, and legislation designed to increase one party's relative share of such massive sums have been a constant feature of managing the flow of royalties from onshore and offshore energy production. Such disputes have invariably been controversial, politically sensitive, and time-consuming for MMS decision makers."

And things become even clearer when we read what the National Commissioners write in the paragraph on

«Agency leadership and technical expertise»:

"Agency personnel naturally look to agency leadership to signal what constitutes their primary mission, including the expertise and experience that such leaders bring with them. In the case of MMS, those signals were profoundly disturbing, yet nonetheless consistent over time. **No one who has led MMS since it was created almost 30 years ago has possessed significant training or experience in petroleum engineering or petroleum geology, or any significant technical expertise related to drilling safety.**

"In the absence of a clear statement from the top about the necessity for such expertise to ensure drilling safety, **it should be no surprise that MMS personnel have suffered from the loss of essential expertise throughout their ranks. Indeed, the lack of requisite training is abysmal. According to a recent survey conducted at the request of the Secretary of the Interior, "[a] lmost half of the [MMS] inspectors surveyed do not believe they have received sufficient training." MMS, unlike Interior's Bureau of Land Management (which inspects onshore oil and gas drilling operations), has no "oil and gas inspection certification program" and no exam "is required of each inspector in order to** be certified." MMS "does not provide formal training specific to the inspections process, and does not keep up with changing technology. Some inspectors noted that they rely on industry representatives to explain the technology at a facility.

"The Macondo well blowout makes all too clear the cost of such a departure from the standards of excellence that the nation expects from its public servants. As described in Chapter 4, the MMS personnel responsible for reviewing the permit applications submitted to MMS for the Macondo well were neither required nor prepared to evaluate the aspects of that drilling operation that were in fact critical to ensuring well safety. The regulations did not mandate that MMS regulators inquire into the specifics of "rupture disks," "long string" well designs, cementing process, the use of centralizers, lockdown sleeves, or the temporary abandonment procedures (see Chapter 4). And, no doubt for that same reason, the MMS personnel responsible for deciding whether the necessary drilling permits were granted lacked the expertise that would have been necessary in any event to determine the relative safety of the well based on any of these factors." (emphases supplied)

«The Ocean is great!», said Tony Hayward, BP Chief Executive Officer and Top Oil Industry Player. And «Tell me whom I must kick in the ass!», said Barack Obama to a crowd of outraged victims.

«The loss occurred in a large ocean that would seek to disperse the oil»,

said Tony Hayward—as the media reported—BP chief executive officer and one of the oil industry's top players.

In short: "the Ocean is great, and will digest whatever oil spillage we throw at it!". So, don't worry about casings or standard test methods! Let's just do whatever it takes to make the American people believe that America had been made safe from oil pollution, and, when oil pollution happens, leave to the "great" Ocean (helped, may be, by tons of chemicals) to see to the problem of swallowing it!

Is this false? Perhaps! Everything is possible, as my father would have said, in this world of thieves! Even if the «nameplate formula» is a fact, the Deepwater Horizon catastrophe is a fact as well, «the large floating tar-like stains» spread all over the Gulf are facts, the befouled shorelines are facts, the dead animals are facts, the hospitalized workers are facts, the DOT official statements are facts, the missed intervention of MSRC is a fact, and the airplanes spraying immense quantities of chemicals are facts. And also Tony Hayward is a fact.

And I respectfully expect Tony Hayward, or the Hon. Billy Tauzin, to deny them.

In the meantime, I would like to remind people that, chased by a crowd of outraged victims, President Obama said: «Tell me whom I must kick in the ass!», as the media reported.

Well, now he knows! And, now that he knows «whom he must kick in the ass!», I deferentially expect that—aided perhaps by a couple of wrestlers—President Obama will keep his formal and public promise, possibly broadcasting his response live worldwide from the Yankee Stadium with fifty TV crews.

And if, eating his own words, President Obama does not maintain his promise, I hope that those kicks will be administered to him by the American people.

Donald Duck (or Mickey Mouse, if you prefer), after all, is not an oil recovery system!

But let's leave Tony Hayward and President Obama to sleep untroubled, and let's see how, in the words of the National Commissioners, the Marine Spill Response Corporation responded to the Macondo oil spill, and how BP demonstrated its response capacity to the President of the United States.

.

About walruses, the Marine Spill Response Corporation, and «commitments soon forgotten as memories dimmed»

After having stated, in the paragraph entitled "Response and Containment", that

"Although the National Contingency Plan requires the Coast Guard to supervise an oil-spill response in coastal waters, it does not envision that the Coast Guard will provide all, or even most, of the response equipment. That role is filled by private oil-spill removal organizations, which contract with the oil companies that are required to demonstrate response capacity. BP's main oil-spill removal organization in the Gulf is the Marine Spill Response Corporation, a nonprofit created by industry after the Exxon Valdez disaster to respond to oil spills."
(Report to the President, page 132)

the National Commissioners go on to describe how the Marine Spill Response Corporation responded to the Macondo well oil disaster:

"The Marine Spill Response Corporation dispatched four skimmers within hours of the explosion. BP's oil-spill response plan for the Gulf of Mexico claimed that response vessels provided by the Marine Spill Response Corporation and other private oil-spill removal organizations could recover nearly 500,000 barrels of oil per day.
"Despite these claims, the oil-spill removal organizations were quickly outmatched. While production technology had made great advances since Exxon Valdez (see Chapter 2), [American] spill response technology had not. The Oil Pollution Act of 1990, by requiring double hulls in oil tankers, had effectively reduced tanker spills. But it did not provide incentives for industry or guaranteed funding for federal agencies to conduct research on oil-spill response. Though incremental improvements in skimming and boom had been realized in the intervening 21 years, the technologies used in response to the Deepwater Horizon and Exxon Valdez oil spills were largely the same."
(Ibidem, same page)

But, the National Commissioners continue, "If BP's response capacity was underwhelming,"

"some aspects of its response plan were embarrassing. In the plan, BP had named Peter Lutz as a wildlife expert on whom it would

rely; he had died several years before BP submitted its plan. BP listed seals and walruses as two species of concern in case of an oil spill in the Gulf; these species never see Gulf waters. And a link in the plan that purported to go to the Marine Spill Response Corporation website actually led to a Japanese entertainment site. (Congressional investigation revealed that the response plans submitted to MMS by Exxon Mobil, Chevron, Conoco Phillips, and Shell were almost identical to BP's—they too suggested impressive but unrealistic response capacity and three included the embarrassing reference to walruses.)"
(Report to the President, pages 132 and 133)

In short, the same things that the National Commissioners had already said in the paragraph: «Oil Pollution Act of 1990 and Oil Spill Response Plans»:

"Under the Oil Pollution Act of 1990, as supplemented by a Presidential Executive Order, MMS is responsible for oil spill planning and preparedness as well as select response activities for fixed and floating facilities engaged in exploration, development, and production of liquid hydrocarbons and for certain oil pipelines. The agency requires all owners or operators of offshore oil-handling, storage, or transportation facilities to prepare Oil Spill Response Plans.
"MMS regulations detail the elements of the response plan (an emergency-response action plan, oil-spill response equipment inventory, oil-spill response contractual agreements, a calculation of the worst-case discharge scenario, plan for dispersant use, in-situ burning plan, and information regarding oil-spill response training and drills). The emergency response plan is supposed to be the core of the overall plan, and in turn is required to include information regarding the spill-response team; the types and characteristics of oil at the facilities; procedures for early detection of a spill; and procedures to be followed in the case of a spill. But neither BP, in crafting its Oil Spill Response Plan for the Gulf of Mexico applicable to the Macondo[23] well, nor MMS in approving it, evidenced serious attention to detail. For instance,

....
23 Little curiosity: BP had named the prospect Macondo after the fictional town in Gabriel Garcia Márquez's novel One Hundred Years of Solitude.

the BP plan identified three different worst-case scenarios that ranged from 28,033 to 250,000 barrels of oil discharge and used identical language to "analyze" the shoreline impacts under each scenario. To the same effect, half of the "Resource Identification" appendix (five pages) to the BP Oil Spill Response Plan was copied from material on NOAA websites, without any discernible effort to determine the applicability of that information to the Gulf of Mexico. As a result, the BP Oil Spill Response Plan described biological resources nonexistent in the Gulf—including sea lions, sea otters, and walruses."
(Report to the President, pages 83-84)

And again, at page 243:

"Industry's responsibilities do not end with efforts to prevent blowouts like that at the Macondo well. They extend to efforts to contain any such incidents as quickly as possible and to mitigate the harm caused by spills through effective response efforts. As described in Chapter 5, once a spill occurs, the government must be capable of taking charge of those efforts. But government depends upon the resources and expertise of private industry to contain a blown-out well and to respond to a massive subsea oil spill. Chapter 5 also explains how woefully unprepared both government and industry were to contain or respond to a deepwater well blowout like that at Macondo. All parties lacked adequate contingency planning, and neither government nor industry had invested sufficiently in research, development, and demonstration to improve containment or response technology. Notwithstanding its promises in the aftermath of Exxon Valdez that industry would commit significant funds to support more research and development in response technology—through the "Marine Spill Response Corporation," for example—those commitments were soon forgotten as memories dimmed."

CONCLUSION:

"Skimming was less of a success: despite the participation of hundreds of ships and thousands of

people, it collected only 3 percent of the oil."
(Report to the President, page 169)
(And that 3 percent, I add, was recovered with absorbing booms and pads, or even manually with spades and wheel-barrows along the sea-boards.)

And here, I think, we can stop. I believe, in fact, that my remaining readers already have enough material to enable them to draw their own conclusions.

CHAPTER 6

THE COLLATERALS

After having – as politically correct – first of all assured that

> "Even before the spill the Interior Secretary Ken Salazar had been working to remake the agency that regulates offshore oil drilling, the Mineral Management Service",

in article subtitled «The agency has been accused of being too cozy with the industry that it is charged with regulating» Sheryl Gay Stolberg and John M. Broder, contributed by Matthew L. Wald and Brian Knowlton in Washington and Clifford Krauss and Susan Saulny in Houston, on the International Herald Tribune of May 12, 2010 write that

> "It has been caught up in scandals for years, accused to be too cozy with the industry that is charged with regulating.
> "Its current mission includes collecting royalties and negotiating leases even while overseeing safety and environmental protection rules.
> "The agency collects an average of $13 billion a year in royalties and fees from oil and gas on public and Indian lands and offshore."

and that:

> "Mr. Salazar came to the Interior Department last year promising

to clean house at the mineral agency, where officials in the Denver office were found to have accepted **lavish gifts and travel and engaged in sex and drug use with oil company officials.**" (emphasis supplied.)

[...]

"The agency has also historically lacked the staff and the money needed to police the industry.

"Mr. Salazar instituted a new code of conduct for agency officials and halted a royalty program that allowed oil companies to keep billions of dollars that were owed to the government,"

In short, in America there are two types of people: those who have to pay the royalties (or the taxes) due, and those who do not care.

"«They have horribly underestimated the likelihood of a spill and therefore horribly underestimated the consequences of something going wrong» said Robert G. Bea, a professor at the University of California, Berkeley, who studies offshore drilling", James McKinley and Leslie Kaufmann report in the same issue of the International Herald Tribune.

James McKinley and Leslie Kaufmann report in the same issue of the International Herald Tribune.

"The political consequences of the spill in the Gulf of Mexico",

report Peter Baker and Brian Knowlton on the *International Herald Tribune* of May 28, 2010

"continued to reverberate, as the official responsible for overseeing such drilling, S. Elizabeth Birnbaum, stepped down under pressure. Ms. Birnbaum had led the Mineral Management Service since July, but critics said she had done far too little to fix a deeply dysfunctional agency.

"Mr. Obama said that he had learned of her resignation only hours earlier. **He also said that what he called the oil industry's "cozy and sometimes corrupt relationship with government regulators" had resulted in "little or no regulation at all" for years, and he**

vowed to fix that."

According to the National Commissioners all faults originate from the fact that

"Secretary of the Interior James Watt created the agency with great fanfare in January 1982, *aiming from the outset to promote domestic energy supplies by dramatically expanding drilling on the outer continental shelf.* He combined, in one entity, authority for regulatory oversight with responsibility for collecting for the U.S. Treasury the billions of dollars of revenues obtained from lease sales and royalty payments from producing wells. *From birth, MMS had a built-in incentive to promote offshore drilling in sharp tension with its mandate to ensure safe drilling and environmental protection."*
(Report to the President, page 56)

But, as the National Commissioners point out in chapter 3, "It was like pulling teeth", at first MMS carried out its regulatory oversight very scrupulously:

"In carrying out its duties, MMS subjected oil and gas activities to an array of prescriptive safety regulations: hundreds of pages of technical requirements for pollution prevention and control, drilling, well-completion operations, oil and gas wellworkovers (major well maintenance), production safety systems, platforms and structures, pipelines, well production, and well-control and production-safety training. As required by the 1978 Act, MMS also attempted to conduct both annual and periodic unscheduled (unannounced) inspections of all offshore oil and gas operations to try to assess compliance with those requirements. Agency officials have tried to meet the requirement for annual inspections of the operation of safety equipment designed to prevent blowouts, fires, spills, and other major accidents. In both annual and unannounced inspections, MMS officials used a national checklist, covering categories such as pollution, drilling, well completion, production, crane, electrical, and personal safety. Most inspections tend to cover a subset of the elements on the list. **Roughly 20 percent of the matters for inspection (those for the production meters) are not related to safety.**

"But over time, MMS increasingly fell short in its ability to oversee the offshore oil industry. The agency's resources did not keep pace with industry expansion into deeper waters and industry's related reliance on more demanding technologies. And, senior agency officials' focus on safety gave way to efforts to maximize revenue from leasing and production."
(Report to the President, page 68)

... "But", "over time",

"political leaders within both the Executive Branch and Congress failed to ensure that agency regulators have had the resources necessary to exercise that authority"

[...]

"the MMS personnel responsible for reviewing the permit applications submitted to MMS for the Macondo well were neither required nor prepared to evaluate the aspects of that drilling operation that were in fact critical to ensuring well safety. "

and, for obvious and well programmed effect

"senior agency officials' focus on safety gave way to efforts to maximize revenue from leasing and production."

And of this, in addition to the word of the National Commissioners, we have as well the counterproof.

In fact, despite the cancellation of MMS and the reorganization of its missions into three separate entities: a Bureau of Ocean Energy Management; a Bureau of Safety and Environmental Enforcement; and an Office of Natural Resources Revenue, clean up operations carried out after the recent Santa Barbara oil spill[24] have been conducted with buckets and shovels–as we

---

24 On May 19, 2015, an underground pipeline running parallel to a coastal highway inexplicably burst, and 2,500 barrels (105,000 gallons) of crude oil gushed onto San Refugio State Beach and into the Pacific west of Santa Barbara. (Reuters)

all saw on TV in Italy too.

And what else, on the other side, the «officials in the Denver office» could have done if the «political leaders within both the Executive Branch and Congress failed to ensure that agency regulators had the resources necessary to exercise their authority, including personnel and technical expertise, and, no less important, the political autonomy needed to overcome the powerful commercial interests that have opposed more stringent safety regulation»?

On the other hand, not even if we could ask Aristotle and Mr. Gödel for help can we understand how the "responsibility for collecting the billions of dollars from lease sales and royalty payments from producing wells for the Treasury" may contrast with "its mandate to ensure safe drilling and environmental protection." If not in the sense that a more sophisticated regulatory oversight would have entailed more costly and lengthy procedures for research and production.

And it is even harder to see how the Mineral Management Service could oblige industry to increase oil-spill containment and clean up technology, if at any moment oilmen could take the nameplate formula in one hand and the nameplates of their so-called oil recovery devices in the other one and demonstrate to the President of the United States that, *according to the law*, they possessed full capability for responding to an oil spill the size of both the Exxon Valdez and Deepwater Horizon put together.

If «revenue generation—enjoyed both by industry and government» was the dominant objective for both industry and government?

If «there was a hidden price [named loss of human lives and oil pollution] to be paid for those increased revenues» and the «political leaders within both the Executive Branch and Congress» were ready to pay it??

If

"In 2003, the White House stiffly opposed MMS's efforts to update its requirements for the reporting of key risk indicators. (MMS had proposed that all unintentional gas releases be reported, because even small gas leaks can lead to explosions.)

"It was like pulling teeth," one senior MMS official involved with the process told the Commission: "We never got positive cooperation" from either industry or the Office of Management and Budget. The Offshore Operators Committee, an industry association, vehemently objected that the requirement would be too burdensome and not conducive to safety; MMS disagreed, yet the final rule in 2006 mandated that a gas release be reported to MMS only if it resulted in an "equipment or process shut-in," or mechanical closure—a much less complete standard."
(Report to the President, page 72)

If

"During the 1990s, the resources available to MMS decreased precipitously just as it faced a dramatic increase in the offshore activity it was charged with overseeing—and matters only deteriorated thereafter. Perversely, MMS's budget reached its lowest point in November 1996, just as major development activities in deepwater were expanding. That December, the *Houston Chronicle* reported with tragic detail an 81 percent increase in offshore fires, explosions, and blowouts in the Gulf since 1992."
(Ibidem, page 73)

If, as it is apparent from the evidence above, politicians formed the MMS *solely and exclusively to cover their defence of oil companies interests*? If, in short, politicians formed the MMS in order to deceive the American people?

But, apart from offering lavish gifts or making sex and drug use with MMS officials in the Denver office and opposing more stringent safety regulation, busy oilmen had something to sort out in Washington too.

December 29, 2000: The Congress of the United States 'amends' OPA'90

There was in fact yet another money matter.

The Companies «engaged in the handling, storage, and transport of oil and petroleum products» certainly wished to avoid the threat of paying even the moderately severe penalties in terms of civil liability provided for by OPA'90 for any future oil disaster, plainly conscious that some Deepwater Horizon oil catastrophe around the American coasts would sooner or later happen.

And, since «the powerful commercial interests» of the companies «engaged in the handling, storage, and transport of oil and petroleum products» prevail upon the interests of the American people, ten years later, when «the fears and outrage of a nation besieged by oil spills» eventually faded, and the Exxon Valdez disaster was forgotten, the Congress of the United States took pain to «establish limitations on liability for damages» that, in the case of an oil accident, the Companies «engaged in the handling, storage, and transport of oil and petroleum products» could be obliged to pay.

Congress clearly specified this in the very title of the law:

"AN ACT to establish limitations on liability for damages resulting from oil pollution, to establish a fund for the payment of compensation for such damages, and for other purposes."

But let us see what else newspapers and scientists tell us.

The «three dimensional entity» and the «deep, hydrocarbon containing plume at least 22 miles long»

"This leaked oil is a three dimensional entity, and the pictures of it on the surface just depict a very small amount of it. Given the many thousands of square miles of ocean now covered by the slick, that sounds strange, but the total cubic volume is distributed throughout the water column and not visible, and therefore an even more serious issue than realized by many."

BP in order to remove and clean up this "three dimensional entity"

101

"It is not the invasion of Normandy, but by peacetime standards the flotilla stationed about 65km (40 miles) off the Louisiana coast is a mightily impressive one,"

in an unsigned editorial, *The Economist* of May 22, 2010, writes.

But, rather contradictorily *The Economist* continues, to combat this three dimensional entity

"By mid-week some 582,000 gallons of dispersant had been sprayed since the emergency began."

I.e. the «mightily impressive flotilla» stationed off the Louisiana failed to recover anything at all, and the visible part of the three dimensional entity was simply sprayed from airplanes with tons of chemicals and thus hidden from view by being sunk onto the seabed.

Indeed, as the *Economist* reports, «by mid-week some 582,000 gallons of dispersant had been sprayed since the emergency began» and other «45.000 gallons» were injected «into the plume where it leaves the riser».

Right, «by May 22, 2010».

But, how many gallons of chemicals have been sprayed, in total, adding pollution to pollution, on the sea surface and «into the oil plume where it leaves the riser»?

"To combat last year's Deepwater Horizon oil spill,"

Woods Hole Oceanographic Institution (WHOI) reports,

"nearly 800,000 gallons of chemical dispersant were injected directly into the oil and gas flow coming out from the wellhead, nearly one mile deep in the Gulf of Mexico, [...] and 1.4 million gallons of dispersant [were] applied at the ocean surface[25]."
Total: 2.2 million gallons.

But, besides these figures, what were the effects produced by the application of all these chemicals?

....

25 For more information see: (www.whoi.edu) Woods Hole Oceanographic Institution News Release: First Study of Dispersant in Gulf Spill suggests a Prolonged Deepwater Fate.

"A research team led by the Woods Hole Oceanographic Institution (WHOI) has determined what chemicals were contained in a deep, hydrocarbon containing plume at least 22 miles long that WHOI scientists mapped and sampled last summer in the Gulf of Mexico, a residue of the Deepwater Horizon oil spill.

[…]

"In three dives covering 146 miles between June 23 and 27, Sentry [the autonomous underwater vehicle (AUV) used by WHOI scientists to map the plume] sculpted the shape of the plume. It was more than a mile wide and 600 feet high, and it flowed continuously southwest from Deepwater Horizon at a speed of about 4 miles per day for at least 22 miles.

[...]

"The data "provide compelling evidence" that the oil component of the plume sampled in June 2010 essentially comprised benzene, toluene, ethybenzene, and total xylenes—together, called BTEX—at concentrations of about 70 micrograms per liter.

[…]

"[WHOI chemist] Elizabeth B. Kujawinski and her colleagues found one of the dispersant's key components, called DOSS (dioctyl sodium sulfosuccinate), was present in May and June—in parts per-billion concentrations—in the plume from the spill more than 3,000 feet deep.

[…]

"Using a new, highly sensitive chromatographic technique that she and WHOI colleague Melissa C. Kido Soule developed, Kujawinski reports those concentrations of DOSS indicate that little or no biodegradation of the dispersant substance had occurred. The deep-water levels suggested any decrease in the compound could be attributed to normal, predictable dilution. They found further evidence that the substance did not mix with the 1.4 million gallons of dispersant applied at the ocean surface and appeared to have become trapped in deepwater plumes of oil and natural gas reported previously by other WHOI scientists and members of this research team. The team also found a striking relationship between DOSS levels and levels of methane, which further supports their assertion that DOSS became trapped in the subsurface.

[…]

"With this method, we were able to tell how much [dispersant] was there and where it went," Kujawinski said. She and her colleagues detected DOSS up to around 200 miles from the wellhead two to three months after the deep-water injection took place, indicating the mixture was not biodegrading rapidly.

[...]
"Over 290,000 kg, or 640,000 pounds, of DOSS was injected into the deep ocean from April to July," she said. "That's a staggering amount, especially when you consider that this compound comprises only 10% of the total dispersant that was added.
[...]
"Kujawinski cautioned that "we can't be alarmist" about the possible implications of the lingering dispersant. Concentrations considered "toxic" are at least 1,000 times greater than those observed by her and her colleagues, she said. But because relatively little is known about the potential effects of this type of dispersant/hydrocarbon combination in the deep ocean, she added, "We need toxicity studies."

In short: part of the «nearly 800,000 gallons of chemical dispersant injected directly into the oil and gas flow coming out from the wellhead» and part of «the oil and gas flow coming out from the wellhead» «were swept away laterally by prevailing ocean currents, and remained trapped in deepwater plumes», while the oil that did nevertheless reach the sea surface was sunk on the sea floor by the 1.4 million gallons of dispersant applied at the ocean surface.

(The findings of this interesting search are published in the online edition of the Proceedings of the National Academy of Sciences.)

"We need toxicity studies."

The data reported by WHOI scientists automatically lead back, as Kujawinsky says, to the more than obvious question: how toxic are the 2.2 million gallons[26] of dispersant applied to the Gulf of Mexico?

Nobody knows!

All we know is that the dispersants used by BP were, almost exclusively, the Corexit 9500, the Corexit 9527 or possibly the Corexit EC9500A produced by Nalco.

But no one knows the formula of these Corexit.

....
26 Which I do believe are minimized, considered that – as WHOI reports – the «over 290,000 kg» of the DOSS injected only represent «10% of the total dispersant that was added.»

104

Notwithstanding all the Public Laws that have forced even the Coca Cola Company to reveal the formula of its world-famous drink, Nalco has never revealed the formula of Corexit. Or, more precisely, Nalco has never been obliged to reveal the formula of Corexit.

So, the only thing we know about Corexit is the information that Nalco itself has spontaneously decided to give us: the ten pages of Material Safety Data Sheet (MSDS), for instance, reported by Nalco on its website (lmrk.org/corexit_9500_uscueg.539287.pdf) on Corexit 9500, where, under section 15: «Regulatory Information», they write (don't bother to read, in full, all the writing below, just try to read between the lines):

//

NATIONAL REGULATIONS, USA :
OSHA HAZARD COMMUNICATION RULE, 29 CFR 1910.1200 :
Based on our hazard evaluation, the following substance(s) in this product is/are hazardous and the reason(s) is/are shown below.

Distillates, petroleum, hydrotreated light: Irritant
Propylene Glycol: Exposure Limit, Eye irritant
Organic sulfonic acid salt: Irritant

CERCLA/SUPERFUND, 40 CFR 117, 302 :
Notification of spills of this product is not required.
SARA/SUPERFUND   AMENDMENTS   AND REAUTHORIZATION ACT OF 1986 (TITLE III) - SECTIONS 302, 311, 312, AND 313 :
SECTION 302 - EXTREMELY HAZARDOUS SUBSTANCES (40 CFR 355) :
This product does not contain substances listed in Appendix A and B as an Extremely Hazardous Substance.

SECTIONS 311 AND 312 - MATERIAL SAFETY DATA SHEET REQUIREMENTS (40 CFR 370) :
Our hazard evaluation has found this product to be hazardous. The product should be reported under the following indicated EPA hazard categories:
        X Immediate (Acute) Health Hazard
        - Delayed (Chronic) Health Hazard
        - Fire Hazard

- Sudden Release of Pressure Hazard
- Reactive Hazard

SECTION 313 - LIST OF TOXIC CHEMICALS (40 CFR 372):
This product does not contain substances on the List of Toxic Chemicals.

TOXIC SUBSTANCES CONTROL ACT (TSCA) :
The substances in this preparation are included on or exempted from the TSCA 8(b) Inventory (40 CFR 710)

FEDERAL WATER POLLUTION CONTROL ACT, CLEAN WATER ACT, 40 CFR 401.15 / formerly Sec. 307, 40 CFR 116.4 / formerly Sec. 311:
None of the substances are specifically listed in the regulation.

CLEAN AIR ACT, Sec. 111 (40 CFR 60, Volatile Organic Compounds), Sec. 112 (40 CFR 61, Hazardous Air Pollutants), Sec. 602 (40 CFR 82, Class I and II Ozone Depleting Substances):
None of the substances are specifically listed in the regulation.
Substance(s) Citations
• Propylene Glycol Sec. 111

CALIFORNIA PROPOSITION 65 :
This product does not contain substances which require warning under California Proposition 65.

MICHIGAN CRITICAL MATERIALS:
None of the substances are specifically listed in the regulation.

STATE RIGHT TO KNOW LAWS:
The following substances are disclosed for compliance with State Right to Know Laws:
Propylene Glycol 57-55-6

NATIONAL REGULATIONS, CANADA:
WORKPLACE HAZARDOUS MATERIALS INFORMATION SYSTEM (WHMIS):
This product has been classified in accordance with the hazard criteria of the Controlled Products Regulations (CPR) and the MSDS contains all the information required by the CPR.

WHMIS CLASSIFICATION:
Not considered a WHMIS controlled product.

CANADIAN ENVIRONMENTAL PROTECTION ACT (CEPA):

The substances in this preparation are listed on the Domestic Substances List (DSL), are exempt, or have been reported in accordance with the New Substances Notification Regulations.

"

Wonderful! Delightful! «This product does not contain substances which require warning under California Proposition 65» and «none of the substances are specifically listed in the Clean Air Act, Sec. 111, 112 and 602».

But: having told us what substances Corexit 9500 does not contain, or are not specifically listed in the Michigan Critical Materials Regulations, when will Nalco, at long last, finally inform us what substances Corexit 9500 contains? Or will somebody (the President of the United States, for example) analyze this product sprayed in massive amounts over the Caribbean Sea and beneath it, and eventually tell us, exactly, what it contains, and whether or not it is dangerous for human health? And also whether the *Corexit-oil mixture* is dangerous for human health?

We need to know this because it doesn't appear that what Nalco writes is true (or at least there are good reasons for not believing them).

According to a report by David Kirby for TakePart, the main component of the Corexit formula used during cleanup, 2-butoxyethanol, was identified as "one of the agents that caused liver, kidney, lung, nervous system, and blood disorders among cleanup crews in Alaska following the 1989 Exxon Valdez spill."

I read in Wikipedia that Susan Shaw, an American environmental health scientist, explorer and ocean conservationist, predicted the decimation of deep-water coral, a species known to be sensitive to the Corexit-oil mixture, and the deaths of dolphins from unavoidable inhalation of the mixture as they surfaced to breathe. Both outcomes have since occurred. She also predicted the human health crisis in the Gulf today with a high level of certainty, stating that a scientific review found that "five of the Corexit ingredients are linked to cancer, 33 are associated with skin irritation from rashes to burns, 33 are linked to eye irritation, 11 are or are suspected of being potential respiratory toxins or irritants, and 10 are suspected kidney toxins."

CONCLUSION

The President of the United States has allowed the massive use of a product the formula of which is unknown. Or, to put it another way, without even knowing which substances he permitted to use of.

But did the technology really exist that would have actually cleaned-up, «to the maximum practicable extent», the Exxon Valdez, the Deepwater Horizon oil catastrophes, and all the «thousands of spill» which, as NRDC reports, «continue to occur routinely in U.S. waters»?

A basic and very intriguing question, which requires an answer.

CHAPTER 7

FROM THE 1980s THE CONGRESS OF THE UNITED STATES, THE REGULATORY AGENCIES AND THE OIL INDUSTRY KNEW VERY WELL THAT DEVICES REALLY CAPABLE OF RECOVERING FLOATING OILS EXISTED

Intrigued by the oil pollution recovery problem, mainly because it was an unsolved issue, in the late 1970s and the early 1980s I designed, at my own expense, a complete line of vessels and oil removal devices which, tested under ASTM F 631 – 80 Standard test method by

- the European Economic Community within the framework of the 1984 EEC pilot-scheme "Recovery of heavy oils in open seas";
- the Technical Inspectorate (IT) of the Italian Ministry for the Merchant Navy;
- the Italian National Institute for Naval Architecture Studies and Experiences (INSEAN);
- the Lloyd's Register and
- the Italian Experimental Station for Fuels

proved—see documents from 9 to 14—**capable of mechanically recovering spilled oils at an Oil Recovery Rate (ORR) up to 22.6 m³/h (i.e. 45.2 m³/h, since a vessel can operate 2 devices) with a Recovery Efficiency (RE) ranging from 0,72 up to 0,91.**

Moreover these devices have proved to be capable of recovering, even if at greatly reduced Oil Recovery Rates, also oil-in-water emulsions[27].

---

27 The question, indeed, of the oil-in-water emulsion is a bit complex, and deserves some further investigation.

After a prolonged permanency on sea surface, the oil polluted layer first looses most of its most light parts (methane, gasoline, naphtha, and so on) by evaporation and watering, while, due to Brownian motion and the mechanical action of waves, winds and currents, its remaining and most heavy parts (such as, but not only, asphalt and bitumen) mix inextricably with water and form an emulsion of oil in water (dispersion of infinitesimal droplets of oil in a body of water, in jargon called 'chocolate mousse', perhaps for its brown color), which alternatively shows the physical properties of the oil or of the water.

"Thermal Agitation" and "Surface Tension", "Water Surface Tension", are the responsible for this dramatic change.

What Physicists today call thermal agitation (i.e. the random motion of the molecules of a stationary liquid) was first observed in 1828 by the British naturalist Robert Brown when he noticed, observing the motion of microscopic bits of plant pollen suspended in still water under a microscope, that they exhibited an incessant zigzag motion, as if they were incessantly and randomly hit by millions of invisible bullets.

But in 1828 atoms and molecules were still open to objection, and so they remained until, in 1905, Albert Einstein confirmed the atomic theory of matter with his seminal paper: *On the movement of small particles suspended in a stationary liquid demanded by the molecular-kinetic theory of heat*: "In this paper it will be shown that, according to the molecular-kinetic theory of heat, bodies of a microscopically visible size suspended in a liquid must, as a result of thermal molecular motions, perform motions of such magnitudes that they can be easily observed with a microscope. It is possible that the motions to be discussed here are identical with so-called Brownian molecular motion; however, the data available to me on the latter are so imprecise that I could not form a judgment on the question...".

The issue was eventually solved tree years later, when the Frenchman Jean Perrin (awarded the Nobel Prize for Physics in 1926) verified Einstein predictions in the laboratory. Wilhelm Ostwald, in the fourth edition of his treatise on general chemistry, honestly admitted: "I am convinced that we have recently come to demonstrate the corpuscular nature of matter, which the atomic hypothesis for centuries, even for thousand years, had tried in vain."

The phenomenon known as surface tension, instead, is determined by the cohesive forces among liquid molecules and by the position of the molecules in the liquid. In fact, while in the bulk of a liquid each molecule, surrounded on all sides by other molecules, is pulled in every direction, resulting in a force of zero, the boundary molecules, surrounded only on one side by other molecules, are only pulled inwards, while surface molecules attract each other as a result of the horizontal forces. This

110

Fully convinced (aarrrggghhhh) that everybody in the USA would enthusiastically welcome the solution to the problem of oil spills removal (and fully believing, at that time, that America gives anybody a chance), I went to the USA in the early 1980s and started an intense and extremely expensive commercial-cum-information campaign. And, the better to carry on my campaign (let's say, like a quasi-American), I also founded an American Company, the[28] Endtech, Environmental Defense Technologies (see document 15) Inc. in Wilmington, Delaware.

I cannot, obviously, recount here in every detail all the lengths I went to in America to make everybody concerned with the oil pollution problem acquainted with the existence of my vessels and my skimmers.

So I will only say that I went, always at my own expense, all over the United States (New York, Boston, Detroit, Washington, New Orleans, Houston, Providence, Cleveland, Anchorage, San Antonio, Los Angeles, San Francisco, and so on) where I met, practically, all the major public authorities and private operators concerned with the oil pollution recovery problem.

In Leonardo, N.J., moreover, I repeatedly met the chief executive and the technical officers of OHMSETT, and indicated to them my availability and my interest in repeating the tests on my machines according to ASTM F 631 – 80 Standard Test

---

creates some internal pressure and a surface tension (attraction) which forces the liquid surface to the minimal area. In short, surface tension is the force which tends to pull a droplet of water into a spherical shape, and which thereby allows some extremely light species of insects (the *water striders*) to walk freely on the water's surface.

At this point it is also intuitively evident that surface tension, i.e. the force with which the surface molecules bind the water molecules into a droplet, or in a glass of water, is a notably strong force. So that, when the percentage of the oil in an emulsion becomes extremely high and extremely fragmented, the emulsion assumes the shape of infinitesimal droplets of oil 'wrapped' by a thin veil of water which, thanks to its surface tension, keeps the infinitesimal oil droplets tied together in exactly the same way as the veil of sea water keeps the grains of sand tied together at the water edge of a sandy beach.

In short, this is the worst situation you can encounter in an antipollution operation.

28 Still in existence.

Method.

In Washington, D.C., I also contacted the David Taylor Model Basin, to whom I again repeatedly made the same request and indicated my availability but always in vain.

I also attended (with my own stands)

- the first edition of the Business Opportunities Conference (organized by the Association of the USA Governors) in Washington, D.C.,
- one edition of TechEx, The Annual World Fair for Technology Exchange in Atlanta (Georgia);
- one edition of the Offshore Technology Conference in Houston (Texas);
- two editions of PetroEx, always in Houston; and
- two editions of the Oil Spill Conference (the most specialized of the 'Conferences' on oil pollution in the world) that were held, respectively, in San Antonio (Texas) and at the Bonaventure Hotel in Los Angeles (California),

and my Company's name also appeared together with a short description of my vessels and oil removal devices in many technical magazines as well as in the official catalogs of those fairs and conferences.

Furthermore, I personally met with the officials of the American Petroleum Institute in New York, of the Environmental Protection Agency in Cincinnati (Ohio), of the Coast Guard in Washington, D.C., of the U.S. Navy in Groton (R.I.) and of the Marine Spill Response Corporation itself again in Washington, D.C.

Thus, right from the early 1980s every single American concerned with the oil pollution problem was very well aware that the technology capable of removing «to the maximum practicable extent», both the pollution caused by the Exxon Valdez to the Prince William Sound and by the Deepwater Horizon to the Caribbean Seas—not to mention the «thousands of spills» that each year routinely occur along the American coasts and inland waters—existed and was available.

The lobbying activity I performed before the House

Subcommittee on Coast Guard and Navigation and the U.S. Coast Guard

But in the USA I did not only inform Oilmen and the Regulating Agencies of the existence of my vessels and oil removal devices.

In fact, once I realized that

a) <u>Intentionally betraying the American people</u>, the companies «engaged in the handling, storage, and transport of oil and petroleum products» were *criminally* determined to base the defense of the American waters against oil spills on those same identical vessels and those same identical devices that «failed miserably» in Alaska, and that,

b) <u>Intentionally betraying the American people</u>, the Congress of the United States was *criminally* determined to adopt the lunatic «nameplate formula» as the Official American Method for «Determining Effective Daily Recovery Rate for Oil Recovery Devices»,

I contacted the lobbyists David W. Burgett and James D. Freeman of the Hogan & Hartson Law Firm at the suggestion of my American patent office (Rothwell & Brown), and asked them to indicate to Congress and to the Regulatory Agencies the monstrous nature of the "nameplate formula" and the advisability of adopting, as a reliable index of the performing capacity of oil removal devices, the numerical data experimentally measured, under ASTM F 631 – 80 Standard Test Method, at the OHMSETT facility or other equivalent test tank.

The <u>extremely correct and efficacious</u> lobbyists Burgett and Freeman accepted this task, and, on the occasion of the *Hearing on the Implementation of Section 4202(a)(6) of the Oil Pollution Act of 1990 Requiring Oil-carrying Vessels to Carry Discharge Response Equipment* held on February 17th and March 18th, 1993, before the House Subcommittee on Coast Guard and Navigation, they presented, on my behalf, a «written testimony» to the House Subcommittee and a «communication» to the «Executive Secretary, Marine Safety Council, U.S. Coast Guard Headquarters» (both published by the U.S. Government Printing Office, see Documents 3, 4 and 5), wherein, after having well premised that

> "Endtech designs oil skimming equipment and vessels that, unlike other currently available skimmers, are capable of being operated in open seas under less-than-ideal conditions"

and that

> "Key aspects of Endtech's skimmer designs have already been tested by official bodies of certification such as Lloyd's Register and the Italian National Institute for Naval Architecture Studies and Experiences."

they also indicated the many advantages and benefits that would derive from the introduction of objective standards, and the misleading consequences caused by a standard information based on the nameplate formula:

> "The introduction of objective standards would also create market-based incentives to improve discharge removal technologies. When faced with competing technologies, the oil transport industry would be more likely to purchase equipment that has been determined to be the most effective in real-world conditions. This would create a corresponding incentive for the discharge removal industry to develop new removal systems and improve existing equipment.
> "Finally, the existence of objective standards would enable a more honest valuation of oil spill response capabilities. As the Coast Guard's proposed and interim final regulation implementing the Oil Pollution Act now stand, skimmer effectiveness may be measured by the removal capacity stated on the skimmer nameplate. However, the nameplate capacity is not based on actual test results under realistic conditions, but on theoretical maximum throughput, which is likely to overstate real performance by many times. Thus, the removal capacity listed on skimmer nameplates does not reflect skimmers' true capabilities. The misleading removal capacity information on skimmer

nameplates has two consequences. First, vessel owners and other spill response authorities have much smaller true response capacities than reliance on nameplate capacity would indicate. Second, vessel owners and other spill response authorities cannot easily determine whether one type of removal equipment will be more successful at removing spilled oil under real-world conditions than another. These shortcomings are not cured by the application of an arbitrary "efficiency factor" of 20%, as provided for in the related vessel response plan interim final rules. See 58 Fed. Reg. 7376, 7413, 7442 (Feb. 5, 1993). Multiplication of a meaningless and unreliable number by this factor simply results in another meaningless figure and fails utterly to distinguish technology that is effective under real conditions from that which is not.

"Accordingly, the Coast Guard's failure to establish objective standards to measure discharge removal capability acts as a disincentive to the development of more efficient removal technology. To ensure that oil spill recovery efforts achieve the most effective response possible, the Coast Guard should establish objective test standards and require vessel response plans and area contingency plans to use the on-water removal equipment that achieves the best test results. Only then would the Coast Guard meet the congressional objectives of the Oil Pollution Act."

Simply perfect!

But congressmen and oil industry players were determined to continue to use those same ships and those same machines that had "failed miserably" both in Alaska and in the Gulf (and later also in California). In a word, they just wanted to continue cheating the American people.

That was why a rule which would distinguish technology that is effective under real conditions from technology which is not effective did not suit them.

And in fact, despite all the efforts of my two excellent lawyers, this ludicrous figure, the «result of the multiplication of a meaningless and unreliable number by an arbitrary efficiency factor», has been *criminally* maintained by the Congress of the United States as the American Standard Method «to distinguish technology that is effective under real conditions from that which is not».

And here I stop.

However, since I don't want anyone to think that I blame the American authorities of all possible misdeeds and forget that in Italy our own government and our bureaucrats have done even worse things, I will give below a partial summary of the unethical acts for the sake of theft for which the Italian government and bureaucrats are responsible here in Italy.

But this will be the subject of the afterword.

AFTERWORD

PART 1

THE OIL POLLUTION BUSINESS IN ITALY: THE CAMORRA, MONEY AND BRIBES.

Swindles are not, of course, an exclusive American scenario.

In Italy, land of the Mafia and the Camorra, the need to defend the sea against oil pollution has been, by Law 31 December 1982 no. 979, removed from the untouchable oilmen (i.e. from the untouchable people who caused that pollution, and the consequent financial damages) and allocated to the State. In short, has been "nationalized". And, at least as regards the financial side of the matter (the money, in short) the incumbency was, as usual, placed to those who suffered those damages.

And, once "nationalized", has become the land of theft for ministers and bureaucrats. In short, something very similar to what the banks of Chicago became in the days of Dillinger and Al Capone.

In Italy, in fact, the Italian government, *supported by a gang of complicit magistrates*, repeatedly awarded by direct negotiation (i.e. by lying, chea, supported as they were by a gang of complicit magistratesting and intentionally violating endless numbers of laws and regulations) the extremaly lucrative contract to the "thoroughly incompetent"[29] companies Ecolmare and Castalia[30]

....

29 Court of Rome, Civil Proceeding n. 53756 R.G.1991, sentence n. 13660.

30 The only one Company formed by the former Italian First Minister Romano Prodi when he was the President of the Iri Group, the great conglomerate of Italian Public

which were "devoid of adequate organization in the sector"[31]. This after the companies in question had repeatedly paid very large sums of money (and we are talking seriously big money - billions and billions of lire and millions and millions of euro) to a lot of Italian ministers and bureaucrats.

An expert witness called by the Criminal Court of Naples[32] has confirmed the existence of a 'hole' (i.e. an unjustified difference between the total income and the registered expenditures) of **8,434,525,456 Italian Lire** (about 5.000,000 U.S. $), in the book-keeping of the Ecolmare Company.

Two public attorneys, the attorney for Trieste[33] and the attorney for Milan[34], ascertained that the Castalia Company had quietly handed over two bribes of **2,000,000,000 Italian Lire (about 1,500,000 US $)** each to the Italian Ministers for the Merchant Navy **Giovanni Prandini** and **Carlo Vizzini.**

Interrogated in prison[35] by the Judge for Preliminary Investigations **Italo Ghitti**, the managing director of Castalia **Roberto Ferraris**, confessed to having paid a **one billion Italian Lire bribe** to the Secretariats of DC and PSI political parties.

«The phenomenon of corruption within the public administration is so prominent and laden with consequences», writes the Deputy Attorney General of the Court of Auditors[36]

Companies.

31 Ibidem

32 Court of Naples, Criminal proceeding n. 1159/87 r.g.g.i., n. 9897/87 r.g.p.m. (Examining Magistrate Angelo Spirito, Prosecutor Manuela Mazzi)

33 Proxy of Trieste, Examining Magistrate Raffaele Tito, Verbal Questioning of Della Zonca Agostino, «QUESTION OF SO-SAID MINISTRIAL BRIBES»

34 Proxy of Milan, Prosecutor Gherardo Colombo, criminal proceeding n.8655/92/21. Cited in Court of Rome, Criminal proceeding n. 1047/97 R.G.P.M., n. 18/97 R.G. COLL.

35 Court of Milan, criminal proceeding n. 8655/92 R.G. crime reports, Prison of San Vittore, Office of the Judge for Preliminary Investigations Mr. Italo Ghitti, verbal questioning of Mr. Roberto Ferraris, CEO of Castalia Company.

36 The Italian judiciary which, in accordance with Article 100 of the Constitution, "exercises control of legality on the acts of the Government, and also subsequent

Alfredo Lener in pages 201 – 205 of the *Findings on General Account for 2008*[37], «**that we have reasons to fear that its social impact may have a negative effect on the economic development of the country to the extent of close to 50 or 60 billion Euros a year** [about 70 or 80 billion U.S. dollars a year] <u>constituting a really immoral and occult tax paid with money taken from the pockets of our citizens</u>».

Mafia, in short. ***Pure Public Mafia***.

And, at this point, I could even stop. It is perfectly clear by now why the corrupt Ministers Prandini and Vizzini illicitly awarded the lucrative service of the defense of the sea against oil spills to Ecolmare and Castalia Companies despite their being «thoroughly incompetent and devoid of adequate organization in the sector».

To see however in practice *how* in contemporary Italy this **Mafia-like** system works, I just want report two or three highlights from my already quoted book: *L'inquinamento d'oro, come si ruba – anche – sull'emergenza ambientale* (Golden pollution, How they steal – also – on environmental emergencies) which has never been refuted or challenged.

(This is not to speak bad of my country, the country of Archimedes, Virgil, Raphael, Galileo and Saint Francis of Assisi, I am referring to the thieves who rule and who unashamedly despoil the country.)

But, let us begin.

HIGHLIGHT N 1:

How, in 1985, the Minister for the Merchant Navy Carta Gianuario and the Official of the Ministry for the Merchant Navy D'Aniello Felice awarded the lucrative service of the defense of the sea against oil spills to the «thoroughly

---

management of state budgets."

37 In those enormous books with which each year the Court of Auditors communicates to the Parliament its judgment on the financial exercise for the previous year.

incompetent and devoid of adequate organization in the sector» Ecolmare Company

April 10, 1985: The Ecolmare Company performs in the wet-dock (i.e. in the most sheltered area from waves and currents: basically a puddle) of the river port of Fiumicino[38] a "demonstration-performance" of the technical-functional and operating capabilities of its oil removal boat Pelican.

Mr. **Felice D'Aniello**, an official of the Ministry for the Merchant Navy and the promoter of the contract, the Rear Admiral **Marcello Vacca Torelli**, Head of Service Procivilmare (Civil Protection of the Sea) and the Ship's Captain **Renato Ferraro**, Commander of the Maritime District of Rome, later Admiral Commander in Chief of the Italian Coast Guard, attended the demonstration.

July 30, 1985: The Director General Felice D'Aniello by direct negotiation awards the lucrative service of the defense of the sea against oil spills to the Ecolmare Company.

Good. We might think that, since the ministry official D'Aniello Felice has verified on 10th April 1985 that the Pelicans are able to remove oil spills perfectly, he has 'correctly' awarded the lucrative service of the defense of the sea against oil spills to the Ecolmare Company. Good.

But how did it really go, on that April 10, 1985, the demonstration-performance in Fiumicino? This is an inevitable question, in this Italy full of thieves, Christian Democrats and jokers.

We know only too well how things really went.

Because, in fact, "stealing twice over is even better than stealing only once" the owner of the Ecolmare Company Mr. Mariano Pane had stolen public money (20b Lire to be precise) theoretically destined for areas of South Italy hit, in 1980 and 1981,

----

38 The river port, i.e., site near the mouth of the Tiber, the river that runs through Rome.

by a series of terrible earthquakes, on the pretext of defending the sea.

And the Prosecutor of Naples opened a criminal case in the course of which he cross-questioned all the public officials who that famous April 10th attended the demonstration-performance of Fiumicino.

It is enough, then, for us to show here a copy of the Judgment/ Order n. r.g.g.i. 1159/87, n. 9897/87 r.g.p.m. issued on September 26, 1990 by the Tribunal of Naples, Examining Magistrate Mr. **Angelo Spirito**, and make copy and paste:

Testimony of Rear Admiral Marcello Vacca Torelli:

"It was a disaster. We realized that the boat did nothing but suck up water mixed with hydrocarbon, emulsify and reject it under the water surface in a strong jet, the violence of which was such as to make the oil spread beneath the surrounding booms.
"In fact, shortly afterwards the oil rejected by the vessel returned to the surface contaminating the entire port of Fiumicino and tainting the boats moored there. Another Pelican struggled outside the enclosure to prevent the slick from extending further, but in vain."
(Court of Naples, Judgment/ Order cited, page 80)

Testimony of the ship's captain (CP) Renato Ferraro:

"The experiment ended in ridicule and clamorous failure, as the the oil purposely poured into a fence of booms, instead of being cleaned up by the Pelican boat spread throughout the entire port overflowing the fence of booms. The stain spread among the many pleasure boats moored there, dirtying their hulls. Therefore, in the days that followed the same Company, helped by a local clean-up firm, had to provide clean-up services for the contaminated hulls."
(Ibidem, pages 84 and 85)

Testimony of the "experienced sailor" Salvatore Aprea:

"What a useless fucking boat!"
(Ibidem, pages 110 and 111)

Moreover, how could the Pelicans ever recover this spilled oil at sea, if – as everyone at the Ministry knew perfectly well – they had been badly, very badly designed for harvesting only solid pollutants (such as plastic bottles or pieces of wood) in port areas and not for the mechanical recovery of oils or other fluid substances? How could they be expected to operate at sea if they were designed to operate only in port areas and were only able to leave port for one hour and that only in perfectly calm sea conditions?

Somebody might even wonder: but first outsourcing this important and specialized service, in contrast with the law that explicitly envisaged direct management, shouldn't the politicians and bureaucrats concerned with the defense of the sea against oil pollution have asked the opinion of an expert? Or, better still, a pool of experts?

Of course they would have sought the opinion of an expert!

Moreover, the "pool of experts" *specifically charged by ministerial decree to effect binding assessments in the field of ship evaluation and shipbuilding,* that is to say the Technical Inspectorate engineers' offices (I.T.) were right there, on the second floor of the same building of the Ministry of the Merchant Navy. Exactly one floor above Minister Gianuario Carta's office and one floor below the office of the public official D'Aniello Felice.

All it would have taken was for the Minister to pick up the internal phone or knock on the ceiling of his office, or for the public official D'Aniello Felice to stamp on the floor and then lean out of the window for a minute and tell the Head of IT to go to Fiumicino and watch the demonstration-performance of the Pelican boats.

But neither the Minister nor the ministerial official Felice D'Aniello ordered the IT engineers go to watch the demonstration-performance at Fiumicino. As the Head of IT Engineer Umberto Sarno testified before the examining magistrate of Naples:

124

"The comparative-functional examination, the indispensability of which had been raised in their reports of 5.15.1985 and 7.2.1985 was never executed."
(Judgment/ Order cited, page 77)

Conclusion: on July 30, 1985, having carefully sealed the lips of the IT engineers, the *criminal* Minister for the Merchant Navy Carta Gianuario and the even more *criminal* public official D'Aniello Felice — *typical representatives of the Italy infested by Christian Democrats, thieves and jokers* —criminally awarded, by direct negoziation, the lucrative service of the defense of the sea against the oil spills by direct negotiation to the Ecolmare Company, hero of the «ridiculous and clamorous failure» of the «demonstration-performance» at Fiumicino.

HIGHLIGHT N. 2:

The Guardia di Finanza (the Italian Financial Police), the Court of Auditors and Notary Luciano Fabiani of Rome refute the «Illustrious Gentleman, Hon. Eng. Costante Degan, Minister of the Merchant Navy»

June 5, 1987: In a letter (Protocol n. 532) Mr. Emidio Santucci, General Manager of the Castalia Company, «appeals» to the «Illustrious Gentleman, Hon. Eng. Costante Degan, Minister of the Merchant Navy» «for the assignment of the services for the prevention and control of pollution of the sea along the entire national coasts».
July 9, 1987[39]: The Minister of the Merchant Navy Hon. Eng. Costante Degan stresses before the Court of Auditors and the Council of the State the *imperative necessity* of granting

....
39 And that is only one month and four days after the request addressed (by a letter shorter than twenty lines) to the Minister, and when, at least nominally, the sea defense service was still supplied by Ecolmare.

the contract for the defense of the sea against oil spills to the Castalia Company urgently for 'only' 50 billion Italian lire (about 35 million dollars net of revaluation) per year, "because of the peculiarities both subjective and objective of the Company with whom it is intended to deal, whose corporate purpose expresses unique, specialized and exclusive talent for carrying the purposes of Law n. 979 (the law, that is, with which the Italian Parliament had graciously 'nationalized' the service of the defense of the sea)" and on 7.22.87 he granted, by direct negotiation the lucrative contract of the defense of the sea against oil spills to the Castalia Company (or rather: he *tried* to grant, since the Court of Auditors rightly refused the registration of this criminal contract).

To tell the truth: as an Italian citizen I am disgusted to see that I am represented by a delinquent who is capable of making, *for criminal purposes*, an official declaration that is **false** as well as idiot. As, quoting only the official papers, I will immediately prove.

On the 12th sheet of the Judicial Police Report no. 41678/VII/1[a] sent on December 9, 1988, by the Guardia di Finanza (the Italian Financial Police) to the Court of Rome (i.e. on a document requested by the Court of Rome itself), Major **Mauro Santonastaso**, Marshal **Giovanni Bruno** and Brigadier **Ferdinando D'Urso** write:

> "On December 10, 1987 [...] the last paragraph [in the bylaws of the Castalia Company] was amended by adding «as well as the activities provided for by law December 31, 1982 n. 979.»"

And, as it were not enough, on the following 13th sheet Major Mauro Santonastaso, Marshal Giovanni Bruno and Brigadier Ferdinando D'Urso stress the point:

> "On page 5 of the agreement, the following consideration of the Castalia company appears: "a Company uniquely qualified in

the defense against pollution of the sea." **That assumption raises concern when you consider that the Castalia was incorporated on July 22, 1986 and has a rather general corporate purpose (it will, as already stated, be integrated on December 1987 when the signing of the convention already took place) does not have the requested means…"**

Unable, in spite of all my good predisposition, to believe such an extraordinary denial, I obtained from the Naples Chamber of Commerce a copy of the *"Verbale dell'«assemblea straordinaria a rogito notaio Luciano Fabiani di Roma rep. n. 20804 della Castalia – Società Italiana per l'Ambiente S.p.A.»"* ("Notary Luciano Fabiani of Rome, Minutes of the «extraordinary gathering rep. n. 20804 of the Castalia Company»"), and I was thus able to verify that, as he had diligently informed the Guardia di Finanza, on December 10, 1987 (i.e. 4 months and 17 days *after* the signing of the convention) the Castalia company had actually added to "the last paragraph of point 4" of its "rather general corporate purposes" the wording:

"the Company may then also perform the activities provided for by law December 31, 1982 no. 979."

May I, at this point, honestly say that the «Illustrious Gentleman Hon. Eng. Costante Degan» was a *natural born forger*, and that Castalia is *a **mafia-like State** company*? An idiot Company of State expressly formed by the then President of IRI (the largest conglomerate of Italian public companies) and in a few years the President of the Italian Government Prof. Romano Prodi for profiting on public contracts?

And at this point I might as well close the discussion. I think, in fact, I have already more than abundantly demonstrated of what lurid pulp are made the idiotic Companies Ecolmare and Castalia and the politicians who by cheating, defrauding and stealing illegally granted them the lucrative contract of the defense of the sea.

But still it lacks the "stone guest": the *Deus ex Machina* that all these frauds has made possible. The Judiciary. Or rather, that small group of magistrates-carrion who, stinking lying and cheating and blatantly betraying their institutional mandate criminally sent to the archives all the hyper documented complaints that I have presented.

I add, therefore, an ultimate highlight and demonstrate this as well.

HIGHLIGHT N. 3:

The "Court of Ministers" of Rome acquits the criminal Minister for the Merchant Navy Gianni Prandini.

With Judgment n. 41/89 Coll, 1683/89C RGPM the "Court of Ministers"[40] of Rome (President Zucchini Paolo, Judges La Greca Sebastiano and Bucarelli Vittorio) has «placed in the archives» – I will try to be brief – the «various complaints» lodged «with effect from 2.17.1988 by Giuseppe Ayroldi against Senator Giovanni Prandini, Minister for the Merchant Navy pro-tempore» because

"the investigation carried out by the administrative authorities before the conclusion of the convention and in context of the same, shows that the public administration is oriented to facing in the shortest time possible objective emergencies for which nothing had previously been seriously attempted, proceeding first to the evaluation of technical competence, both in terms of the equipment to be employed and in terms of the programming of operations, of those Companies in the sector, which had offered an accomplished picture of their abilities."

And I openly say that the magistrates Paolo Zucchini, Sebastiano La Greca and Vittorio Bucarelli are magistrates **extremely 'fanciful'. Or, to put it bluntly, extremely tricksters.**

Only a judge (or a gang of judges) who is criminally

----

40 The Court that investigates the trials of the Ministers of the Italian Government for offenses committed in the exercise of their functions.

determined to cover up a gang of politicians and bureaucrats who have merrily made off with a cartload of millions could

a) speak of "various complaints" in a generic way without specifying what the "various complaints" I had put forward were, and

b) say that "the public administration was facing in the shortest time possible objective emergencies for which previously nothing had been seriously attempted", when the law is dated December 31, 1982, and the contract which formed the object of my «various complaints» was dated 1987.

Obviously I know and yet don't know (that is to say I do know but I have to keep quiet because I don't have proof) why the Magistrates Zucchini Paolo, La Greca Sebastiano and Bucarelli Vittorio were so desirous of covering up the lies and thefts behind the concession of the lucrative sea defence contract to the dumb companies Ecolmare and Castalia.

I will just put this judgment alongside the relevant documentation (drawn entirely from the documentation lined up by the judicial authorities, thus having value as evidence) which I had attached to what Judge Zucchini generically terms my "various complaints" and leave my courteous readers to draw their own conclusions:

> "It is telling that the aforesaid Inspectorate[41] failed in the execution of surveys designed to ascertain the technical capacity of the Castalia equipment because of a lack of funds, see letter no. 7/25/4553 of 10.26.87 (encl. 9)"

writes the *Guardia di Finanza* on page 13 of the already mentioned judicial report no. 41678/VII/1 requested by the Court of Rome.

> "Concerning the content of the new complaint of Ayroldi, it is believed that the most relevant aspect is still connected to the reliability of the equipment offered, or rather *raked on the market* by Castalia Group. In particular, as already described in the

[41] I.e. the above cited Technical Inspectorate of the Ministry of the Merchant Navy.

following report (see page 13), **no specific inspections have been carried out to ascertain the technical suitability of the above mentioned equipment**." (emphases supplied)

the *Guardia di Finanza* points out again on page 2 of the «Continuation of the Report no. 41678/VII/1 of 12.9.88».

And this is not all!

The *Guardia di Finanza* notifies the Court of Rome in the same «Continuation Report no. 41678/VII/1 of 12.9.88» that:

"The Court of Auditors, by letter no. 198 of 12.8.88, declares: "the attached complaint arrived at this office and is passed on for appropriate knowledge, with a request for clarification.

"In particular, doubts having been raised about the capability of the boats used in the context of the Castalia Convention and on the investigations that the Ministry asserts to have performed in execution of the convention itself, we hereby request pertinent information in order to guarantee that payments arranged are made in the certain knowledge that the required conditions of legality have been met."

In short, the Italian Financial Police clearly informs the Court of Rome three times (and reporting, also, the clarification requested by the Court of Auditors) that «**no specific surveys have been conducted to ascertain the suitability of the equipment offered, or rather *raked on the market*, by Castalia Group.**»

The President of the "Court of Ministers" Paolo Zucchini, however, «given the *various acts* relating to the complaints submitted with effect from 2.17.1988 by Giuseppe Ayroldi against Sen. Giovanni Prandini, Minister for the Merchant Navy pro-tempore», «ordered the documents to be filed in the archives» because

"**the investigation carried out by the administrative authorities before the conclusion of the convention and in context of the same, shows that the public administration is oriented to facing in the shortest time possible objective emergencies for which nothing had previously been seriously attempted, proceeding** first to the evaluation of technical competence, both in terms of the equipment to be employed and in terms of the programming of operations, of those Companies in the sector, which had offered an accomplished picture of their abilities."

Never mind that, in a letter (Protocol no. 7/25/1623) on the subject of: «Offers for services for prevention and control of pollution of the sea» sent on May 18,1987, «To the Central Inspectorate for the Defense of the Sea» and to the Cabinet of the Minister, Eng. Umberto Sarno, Head of the Technical Inspectorate of the Ministry for the Merchant Navy gave evidence that:

"Technical examination has proved to be quite difficult, especially for the service within six miles, because of the variety of equipment offered and the vagueness of the descriptions, which do not always allow a full understanding of the functioning of the system used for the removal and separation of pollutant oils. **"In this regard we propose that the convention should contain a clause according to which the results attained by the company need to be verified by a Supervisory Committee which must comprise at least one member of the I.T., in order to verify the technical-functional-operational capabilities of the said equipment, since to date it has only been possible to evaluate from documents and statements made by the interested party. The Commission should be able to propose structural modifications and changes to the equipment provided without the Companies being able to submit claims for additional charges, and allowing for termination of the agreement without claims for damages from the contractors."** (emphasis supplied)

To the President of the Court of Ministers Zucchini Paolo

"the investigation carried out by the administrative authorities before the conclusion of the convention and in context of the same, shows that the public administration is oriented to facing in the shortest time possible objective emergencies for which nothing had previously been seriously attempted, proceeding first to the evaluation of technical competence, both in terms of the equipment to be employed and in terms of the programming

131

of operations, of those Companies in the sector, which had offered an accomplished picture of their abilities."

Never mind that Engineer Sarno has, with the commendable care of a correct and precise technician, further stated that

"Even for the equipment employed beyond six miles the evaluation of suitability has been given on the basis of indications of retrofitting still to be performed, on the presumable condition of use because, in most cases, they are units of the traditional type, especially tugs for the salvage service, supply vessels for supporting the platforms, and evaluation is based on statements by the RINA on the feasibility of the works still to be done."

According to the Magistrate Zucchini Paolo,

"the investigation carried out by the administrative authorities before the conclusion of the convention and in context of the same, shows that the public administration is oriented to facing in the shortest time possible objective emergencies for which nothing had previously been seriously attempted, proceeding first to the evaluation of technical competence, both in terms of the equipment to be employed and in terms of the programming of operations, of those Companies in the sector, which had offered an accomplished picture of their abilities."

Never mind that, with Resolution no. 65/93, the Court of Auditors refused to register, **because it had 9 "profiles of illegitimacy"**, the lavish contract that the Minister for the Merchant Navy **Carlo Vizzini** *tried to award* to the criminal Castalia Company *__after having received a bribe of 2.000.000.000 (or 2.500.000.000) Italian Lire__*.

To the President of the Court of Ministers Zucchini Paolo

"the investigation carried out by the administrative authorities before the conclusion of the convention and in context of the same, shows that the public administration is oriented to facing in the shortest time possible objective emergencies for which nothing had previously been seriously attempted, proceeding first to the evaluation of technical competence, both in terms of

the equipment to be employed and in terms of the programming of operations, of those Companies in the sector, which had offered an accomplished picture of their abilities."

Never mind that in "profile of illegitimacy no. 4" of the afore-mentioned Resolution the Court of Auditors observed that:

"really the examination of each single technical report - sent in response to the remarks - highlights deficiencies that should have prevented the signing of the contract."

According to the Magistrate Zucchini Paolo, however,

"the investigation carried out by the administrative authorities before the conclusion of the convention and in context of the same, shows that the public administration is oriented to facing in the shortest time possible objective emergencies for which nothing had previously been seriously attempted, proceeding first to the evaluation of technical competence, both in terms of the equipment to be employed and in terms of the programming of operations, of those Companies in the sector, which had offered an accomplished picture of their abilities."

Never mind that on 10.26.1987 the Head of the Technical Inspectorate Eng. Umberto Sarno *"felt compelled"* to send to the Cabinet of the Minister, to the Central Inspectorate for the Defense of the Sea and to the Coast Guard a letter protocol no. 7/25/4553

"to point out that to date it is not yet possible to give effect to the instructions issued by the Hon. Minister about the inspections to ascertain the technical suitability of CASTALIA's equipment.
"Despite the constant and repeated concern, we have not yet managed to have the coverage of expenditure for the conduct of operations, and the anticipation of the same.
"The competent Department declared that no instructions on this matter had been received."

Nothing to be done! As far as the President of the Court of

Ministers is concerned

"the investigation carried out by the administrative authorities before the conclusion of the convention and in context of the same, shows that the public administration is oriented to facing in the shortest time possible objective emergencies for which nothing had previously been seriously attempted, proceeding first to the evaluation of technical competence, both in terms of the equipment to be employed and in terms of the programming of operations, of those Companies in the sector, which had offered an accomplished picture of their abilities."

And here I might as well stop.

I think I have supplied enough material to allow anyone to judge things for themselves.

Anyway, to prevent my benevolent reader from imagining that all the judges of the court of Rome are criminals or at least a gang of useful idiots, I provide the list (and I waste even the bold and some flutters) of the judges that I accuse of being lurid criminals subservient to the lobbies of power:

Garofoli Giovanni; D'Albore Achille; Vecchione Salvatore; Ferrara Giovanni; Saieva Giuseppe; Fasanelli Bruno; Bochicchio Lucio; Mauro Eugenio; De Luca Comandini Raffaele; Maresca Maria Francesca; Scivicco Aldo; Pirro Silvia; Colombo Gherardo; Cascini Giuseppe; Zucchini Paolo: La Greca Sebastiano; Bucarelli Vittorio; Trivellini Antonio; Cialoni Maria Teresa.

---

and then in order to avoid that someone can imagine that, once they snatched the contract the ludicrous Castalia and Ecolmare companies somehow got organized and turned into something at least approximately decent, let's see just how they protected the Italian coastlines and seas.

PART 2

HOW THE OVERPAID COMPANIES ECOLMARE AND CASTALIA PROTECTED THE ITALIAN SEAS AGAINST OIL POLLUTION

On April 11, 1991 the Cypriot tanker Haven exploded in the Gulf of Genoa spilling at sea, according to the database Oil Spills M/B, 134.000 tons of Iranian crude oil. And Castalia was sent to clean up marine and coastal areas affected by this terrible disaster.

So far everything is fine.

The problems come when I read on the *Corriere della Sera* (the oldest and most respected Italian newspaper) of November 11, 1996 that

"an expert testimony on the damages to the environment requested by the Prosecutor reveals: the polluted seabed extends over some hundreds of square kilometers, the enormous quantity of oil is a very serious hazard, hundreds of thousands of people may be affected by cancerous agents through fish or shellfish."

So the highly paid Castalia Company did not recover any of the oil, they just sunk it by means of hidden chemical spraying. And, following such a criminal operation, «hundreds of thousands of people may be affected by cancerous agents through the consumption of fish or shellfish»

By eating, in other words, a good stir-fry or a fillet sole either at home or in restaurants.

And, so as not to leave us even the hope that those experts, cheated out of a mistaken evaluation of indirect measurements, may well be wrong, the *Corrierone* ('The Big Courier', as the Italians affectionately call the Corriere della Sera) tells us that

> "the existence of dangerous deposits has been revealed after the surveys with a small bathyscaphe at 340 and 500 meters of depth; besides the river of oil sediments, tar blocks up to 5 meters high were identified covering the seabed where fish and shellfish have live."

In short, the Court of Genoa experts saw with their own eyes that «enormous quantity of oils» and those «sediments of tar» where «fish and shellfish live»..

In exactly the same way, when, twenty years later, in the night between the 22 and 23 February 2010 the "Lombarda Petroli" (an oil deposit near Milan) released 2,410 tons of oil in the Lambro and Po rivers, Castalia and Ecolmare did not recover any oil, which ended up partly into the aquifers of the Po Valley (and therefore in the eggplants and the peppers that finished up on the tables of the Italians), and party in Adriatic Sea.

And in just the same way, Castalia and Ecolmare, today reunited under the name Associazione Temporanea di Imprese Castalia, never removed the 600 tons of oil spilt into the Polcevera river on 17th April 2016 by the Iplom refinery. (It might be interesting, and even instructive, to note that the disaster originated, as we learn from the inquiry into the environmental disaster by the Genoa Judiciary, from one of the twenty 'critical connections' in the refinery pipes: one of them broke. Because – in words of one syllable – although it was perfectly obvious that one of those critical connections could break, the Iplom oilmen were so sure of their own impunity that they didn't bother to repair them.)

In short, Ecolmare and Castalia were born asinine and have remained asinine.

On the other hand: what does that old saying (I think French) say?

> **"EVEN IF YOU PUT IT ON A GOLDEN THRONE, A FROG IS ALWAYS A FROG."**

And here, although I would still have lots more to say, and many other names to mention, I will stop. I am sure that I have proven more than abundantly how and why a herd of corrupt bureaucrats and politicians awarded the lucrative sea defense service against oil pollution to two extremely stupid and inefficient Companies, protected by another herd of criminal magistrates. And none of them has ever gone to jail.

And if any of them, for example Mr. Romano Prodi, has something to say to me, he knows where to find me.

THE DOCUMENTS

DOCUMENT 1-A

AMERICAN SOCIETY FOR TESTING AND MATERIALS: F 631-80 Standard Test Method for FULL SCALE ADVANCING SPILL REMOVAL DEVICES

Ⓐ ASTM Designation: F 631 – 80

AMERICAN SOCIETY FOR TESTING AND MATERIALS
1916 Race St., Philadelphia, Pa. 19103
Reprinted from the Annual Book of ASTM Standards, Copyright ASTM
If not listed in the current combined index, will appear in the next edition.

Standard Test Method for
FULL SCALE ADVANCING SPILL REMOVAL DEVICES[1]

This standard is issued under the fixed designation F 631: the number immediately following the designation indicates the year of original adoption or, in the case of revision, the year of last revision. A number in parentheses indicates the year of last reapproval.

1. Scope

1.1 This standard provides a method for determining performance parameters of full-scale advancing oil spill removal devices in recovering floating oil when tested in a controlled test facility.

2. Applicable Documents

2.1 *ASTM Standards:*
D 88 Test for Saybolt Viscosity[2]
D 341 Viscosity-Temperature Charts for Liquid Petroleum Products[3]
D 445 Test for Kinematic Viscosity of Transparent and Opaque Liquids (and the Calculation of Dynamic Viscosity)[3]
D 1298 Test for Density, Specific Gravity, or API Gravity of Crude Petroleum and Liquid Petroleum Products by Hydrometer Method[3]
D 2161 Conversion of Kinematic Viscosity to Saybolt Universal Viscosity or to Saybolt Furol Viscosity[2]
D 2904 Practice for Interlaboratory Testing of Textiles[4]
D 2905 Practice for Statements on Number of Specimens Required to Determine the Average Quality of Textiles[4]
D 2906 Practice for Statements on Precision and Accuracy for Textiles[4]

3. Summary of Method

3.1 The spill removal device may be tested in a wave/tow tank or other suitable facility with a controllable test environment. Controlled test variables include device velocity relative to the water velocity, oil properties and slick thickness, wave conditions, and pertinent device variables. It is essential that the device be operated in a steady-state condition during the sampling period when oil encounter rate, recovery rate, recovery efficiency, and device parameters are monitored, measured, and recorded.

4. Significance

4.1 This test method provides quantitative data in the form of oil recovery rates, throughput efficiencies, and oil recovery efficiencies under controlled test conditions. The data can be used for evaluating design characteristics of a particular advancing spill removal device or as a means of comparing two or more devices. Caution must be exercised whenever test data are used to predict performance in actual spill situations as the uncontrolled environmental conditions which affect performance in the field are rarely identical to conditions in the test tank. Other variables such as mechanical reliability, presence of debris, ease of repair, ease of deployment, required operator training, operator fatigue, seaworthiness, and transportability also affect performance in an actual spill but are not measured by this method. These variables should be considered along with the test data when making comparisons or evaluations of advancing spill removal devices.

5. Definitions

5.1 *oil recovery rate*—the volume of oil recovered by the device per unit of time.

[1] This method is under the jurisdiction of ASTM Committee F-20 on Spill Control Systems and is the direct responsibility of Subcommittee F-20.12 on Removal.
Current edition approved Jan. 3, 1980. Published April 1980.
[2] *Annual Book of ASTM Standards*, Part 15.
[3] *Annual Book of ASTM Standards*, Parts 23 and 40.
[4] *Annual Book of ASTM Standards*, Part 32.

5.2 *throughput efficiency*—the ratio, expressed as a percentage, of the volume of oil recovered to the volume of oil encountered.

5.3 *oil recovery efficiency*—the ratio, expressed as a percentage, of the volume of oil recovered to the volume of total fluids recovered.

5.4 *advancing oil spill removal device*—a device that removes spilled oil from the water surface when there is relative motion between the device and the water. The device may move through the surrounding fluid or it may be stationary and the surrounding fluid moved past the device.

5.5 *data collection period*—the period of time during a test run when the performance data is recorded.

5.6 *oil*—the fluid distributed on the water of the test facility and recovered by the spill removal device (see Section 8).

5.7 *oil encounter rate*—the volume of oil per unit time actively directed to the removal mechanism.

5.8 *oil slick thickness*—the average thickness of the oil slick encountered by the test device.

5.9 *full-scale equipment*—equipment of the size that is (or will be) available commercially.

6. Interferences

6.1 The table of results (see 13.1) shall address the possibility of test facility effects. For example, wall effects may interfere hydrodynamically with the device's performance.

7. Test Facilities

7.1 At least two types of test facilities, a wave/tow tank and a current tank, may be used to conduct the test outlined in this method.

7.1.1 *Wave/Tow Tank*—A wave/tow tank has a movable bridge or other mechanism for towing the test device through water for the length of the facility. A wave generator may be installed on one end, or on the side of the facility, or both.

7.1.2 *Current Tank*—A current tank is a water-filled tank equipped with a pump or other propulsion system for moving the water through a test section where the test device is mounted. A wave generator may be installed on this type of test facility.

7.1.3 Other facilities, such as private ponds

or flumes, may also be used, provided the test parameters can be suitably controlled and environmental regulations adhered to.

7.2 Ancillary systems for facilities include but are not limited to, a distribution system for accurately delivering oils to the water surface, skimming systems to assist in cleaning the facility between tests, and adequate tankage for storing the test oils.

8. Test Oils

8.1 Three standard test oils for use with this test method are defined in Appendix X1. These oils cover a wide range of properties and are designated with respect to viscosity and specific gravity as light, medium, and heavy. These oils must be Newtonian fluids and may be crude, refined, or simulant.

8.2 If it is desired to use an oil with properties that do not correspond to a standard test oil, a statement must be made in the table of results (see 13.1) that a standard test oil was not used. This statement must discuss the effect of the nonstandard oil on test data with respect to the probable results using the most similar standard test oil.

8.3 The viscosity of oil varies greatly with temperature. Frequently test oils must be distributed in the test facility at temperatures different from the water temperature. When this occurs, the oil generally will approach the surface water temperature:

8.4 If oils that originally meet the conditions stated in Appendix X1 are reused, their properties may change and should be evaluated prior to reuse.

9. Safety Precautions

9.1 Test operations shall conform to established safety requirements for both test facility operations and oil handling. Particular caution must be exercised when handling flammable or toxic test oils.

10. Test Device

10.1 The test device shall be deployed in accordance with facility operating characteristics. The device must be operated in accordance with the manufacturer's specified operating instructions with respect to mechanical operations and established maintenance routines. Modifications to the device for testing purposes

2

shall follow the manufacturer's recommendations and shall be recorded with the test results.

11. Calibration and Standardization

11.1 At the outset of the test, the independent or control test parameters are selected. Typical test variables include:

Test oils	light, medium, and heavy
Test speed	upper and lower limits and speed increments selected as appropriate
Oil slick thickness	appropriate increments for the device being tested
Wave conditions	wave characteristics of significant height, average length, and period and pattern may be varied as appropriate

12. Procedure

12.1 Prior to the test, select the operating parameters, such as tow speed, wave conditions, test oil, and oil distribution rate. Then prepare the facility and spill removal device for the test run. Occasionally, it may be necessary to preload the device with oil to achieve steady-state operation within a reasonable period of time. Any preload must be carefully measured and discharged into the device. Measure or note immediately prior to each test the following parameters describing ambient conditions:

12.1.1 Air temperature,

12.1.2 Water temperature near the surface,

12.1.3 Wind speed,

12.1.4 Wind direction relative to the test device, and

12.1.5 General weather conditions, for example, rain, overcast, sunny, etc.

12.2 Start the wave generator (if necessary), oil distribution system, tow mechanism or water flow, and the spill removal device to begin a test run. Direct the discharge flow of recovered fluid from the device into a holding tank or back into the test tank out of the device's sweep path during the transient start-up period. After steady-state operation is achieved, monitor the discharge flow to obtain performance data. The discharge may be pumped through a flow meter to obtain a flow rate and sampled periodically to obtain the oil-to-fluid ratio. Alternatively, the discharge may be diverted into calibrated sample tanks from which the flow rate and oil-to-fluid ratio may be determined. In either case, the data collection period begins when sampling starts and ends when sampling stops. During the data collection period or immediately thereafter, measure and record the following parameters:

12.2.1 Oil distribution rate,

12.2.2 Fluid recovery rate (oil and water),

12.2.3 Tow speed or current speed,

12.2.4 Wave characteristics,

12.2.5 Length of the data collection period,

12.2.6 Oil encounter rate, and

12.2.7 Operating parameters of the spill recovery device such as belt speed, weir setting, pump speed, etc.

12.3 At the completion of the data collection period, divert the discharge of the spill removal device back into the holding tank or test tank. Stop the wave generator, tow mechanism or water flow, oil distribution, and spill removal device. Analyze samples of the discharge to determine oil-to-fluid ratio. Analyze samples of the recovered test oil to determine the following:

12.3.1 Specific gravity,

12.3.2 Viscosity,

12.3.3 Surface tension,

12.3.4 Interfacial tension with respect to test tank water, and

12.3.5 Water content.

12.4 Perform the analyses in 12.3 at the surface water temperature or in such a way that the values of these parameters at the surface water temperature can be determined from the analytical data.

13. Calculation or Interpretation of Results

13.1 Prepare a table of results for the test run containing the following entries:

13.1.1 Test identification number,

13.1.2 Date and time of day,

13.1.3 Average speed (tow speed or current speed) during data collection period.

NOTE—This rate is averaged over the data collection period.

13.1.4 Test oil type (light, medium, heavy, or nonstandard).

13.1.5 Oil slick thickness.

13.1.6 For regular waves, include height, average period (or length), and whether head or following. For irregular waves, include significant height, significant frequency, spectral characteristics, and whether head or following.

13.1.7 Oil properties at test temperatures, including specific gravity, viscosity, surface tension, interfacial tension with tank water, and initial water content of oil.

3

145

13.1.8 **Total volume of oil distributed during** data collection period.

13.1.9 **Total volume of oil encountered during** data collection period.

13.1.10 **Total volume of fluid (oil/water) recovered during data collection period.**

13.1.11 **Average oil distribution rate (see Note).**

13.1.12 **Average oil encounter rate (see Note).**

13.1.13 **Average fluid (oil/water) recovery rate (see Note).**

13.1.14 **Average oil recovery efficiency (see Note).**

13.1.15 **Average oil recovery rate (see Note).**

13.1.16 **Average throughout efficiency (see Note).**

13.1.17 **Ambient conditions, including air** temperature, surface water temperature, wind speed, wind direction, and brief statement of weather conditions during test run.

13.1.18 Length of data collection period.

13.1.19 **Volume of oil in device at beginning** of data collection period.

13.1.20 **Volume of oil in device at end of** data collection period.

13.1.21 **Operating parameters of the device** such as belt speed, weir setting, pump speed, etc.

13.1.22 **Brief discussion of interferences or** limiting factors (see 6.1).

13.2 If any of the data required by 13.1 are not applicable to the device being tested, a statement must be included in the table of results describing the reasons for omitting the data.

14. Precision and Accuracy

14.1 Statistical measures of accuracy and precision may be determined that will indicate the reliability of test results as well as the degree of standardization in test procedures. Examples of procedures may be found in Appendix X2.

APPENDIXES
X1. STANDARD TEST OILS

X1.1 General

X1.1.1 The ranges of physical properties for standard test oils will be as outlined in X1.2 through X1.5.

X1.2 Viscosity

X1.2.1 *Light Oil*—3 to 10 cSt (mm²/s) at 60°F (15.6°C).
X1.2.2 *Medium Oil*—100 to 300 cSt (mm²/s) at 60°F (15.6°C).
X1.2.3 Heavy Oil—500 to 2000 cSt (mm²/s) at 60°F (15.6°C).

X1.3 Specific Gravity

X1.3.1 *Light Oil*—0.83 to 0.88.
X1.3.2 *Medium Oil*—0.90 to 0.94.
X1.3.3 *Heavy Oil*—0.94 to 0.97.

X1.4 Surface Tension

X1.4.1 *All Oils*—24 to 34 dynes/cm (mN/m) with distilled water at 77°F (25°C).

X1.5 Interfacial Tension

X1.6 *All Oils*—26 to 32 dynes/cm (mN/m) with distilled water at 77°F (25°C).

X2. DETERMINATION OF PRECISION AND ACCURACY

X2.1 The following properties may be determined by the ASTM standards listed which are considered for use in this method for full scale advancing skimmers:

X2.1.1 *Viscosity*—Methods D 88 and D 445.
X2.1.2 *Specific Gravity*—Method D 1298.
X2.1.3 *Viscosity versus Temperature*—Standard D 341.
X2.1.4 *Viscosity Conversion*—Method D 2161.
X2.1.5 *Interlaboratory Testing*—Practice D 2904.
X2.1.6 *Number of Test Replicates*—Practice D 2905.
X2.1.7 *Precision and Accuracy*—Practice D 2906.

4

146

DOCUMENT 1-B

AMERICAN SOCIETY FOR TESTING AND MATERIALS, SUBCOMMITTEE F20.12 ON REMOVAL, http://www.astm.org/COMMIT/SUBCOMMIT/F2012.htm. List of ASTM Standards for oil spill removal devices.

Subcommittee F20.12 on Removal

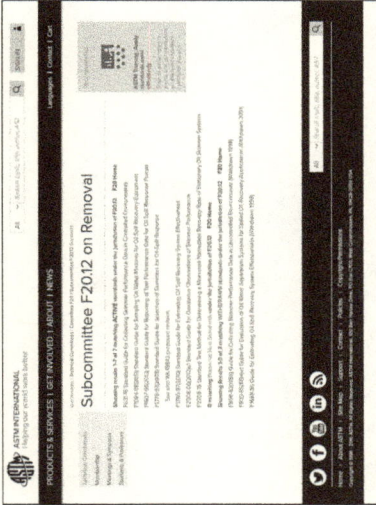

Showing results 1-7 of 7 matching ACTIVE standards under the jurisdiction of F20.12

F631-15 Standard Guide for Collecting Skimmer Performance Data in Controlled Environments

F1084-08(2013) Standard Guide for Sampling Oil/Water Mixtures for Oil Spill Recovery Equipment

F1607-95(2013) Standard Guide for Reporting of Test Performance Data for Oil Spill Response Pumps

F1778-97(2008) Standard Guide for Selection of Skimmers for Oil-Spill Response

   See also WK49843 proposed revision

F1780-97(2010) Standard Guide for Estimating Oil Spill Recovery System Effectiveness

F2008-00(2012)e1 Standard Guide for Qualitative Observations of Skimmer Performance

F2709-15 Standard Test Method for Determining a Measured Nameplate Recovery Rate of Stationary Oil Skimmer Systems

0 matching Proposed New Standards under the jurisdiction of F20.12

Showing Results 1-3 of 3 matching WITHDRAWN standards under the jurisdiction of F20.12

F808-83(1988) Guide for Collecting Skimmer Performance Data in Uncontrolled Environments (Withdrawn 1998)

F933-85(1994)e1 Guide for Evaluation of Oil Water Separation Systems for Spilled Oil Recovery Applications (Withdrawn 2001)

F1688-96 Guide for Estimating Oil Spill Recovery System Effectiveness (Withdrawn 1999)

149

DOCUMENT 2

Oil Pollution Act of 1990: TITLE VII—OIL POLLUTION RESEARCH AND DEVELOPMENT PROGRAM.

SEC. 6002. ANNUAL APPROPRIATIONS.

(a) REQUIRED.—Except as provided in subsection (b), amounts in the Fund shall be available only as provided in annual appropriation Acts.

(b) EXCEPTIONS.—Subsection (a) shall not apply to sections 1006(f), 1012(a)(4), or 5006, and shall not apply to an amount not to exceed $50,000,000 in any fiscal year which the President may make available from the Fund to carry out section 311(c) of the Federal Water Pollution Control Act, as amended by this Act, and to initiate the assessment of natural resources damages required under section 1006. Sums to which this subsection applies shall remain available until expended.

(33 U.S.C. 2752)

〖Section 6003—Repealed by section 109 of P.L. 104–134〗

SEC. 6004. COOPERATIVE DEVELOPMENT OF COMMON HYDRO-CARBON-BEARING AREAS.

(a) * * *

(b) EXCEPTION FOR WEST DELTA FIELD.—Section 5(j) of the Outer Continental Shelf Lands Act, as added by this section, shall not be applicable with respect to Blocks 17 and 18 of the West Delta Field offshore Louisiana.

(c) AUTHORIZATION OF APPROPRIATIONS.—There are hereby authorized to be appropriated such sums as may be necessary to provide compensation, including interest, to the State of Louisiana and its lessees, for net drainage of oil and gas resources as determined in the Third Party Factfinder Louisiana Boundary Study dated March 21, 1989. For purposes of this section, such lessees shall include those persons with an ownership interest in State of Louisiana leases SL10087, SL10088 or SL10187, or ownership interests in the production or proceeds therefrom, as established by assignment, contract or otherwise. Interest shall be computed for the period March 21, 1989 until the date of payment.

TITLE VII—OIL POLLUTION RESEARCH AND DEVELOPMENT PROGRAM

SEC. 7001. OIL POLLUTION RESEARCH AND DEVELOPMENT PROGRAM.

(a) INTERAGENCY COORDINATING COMMITTEE ON OIL POLLUTION RESEARCH.—

(1) ESTABLISHMENT.—There is established an Interagency Coordinating Committee on Oil Pollution Research (hereinafter in this section referred to as the "Interagency Committee").

(2) PURPOSES.—The Interagency Committee shall coordinate a comprehensive program of oil pollution research, technology development, and demonstration among the Federal agencies, in cooperation and coordination with industry, universities, research institutions, State governments, and other nations, as appropriate, and shall foster cost-effective research mechanisms, including the joint funding of research.

(3) MEMBERSHIP.—The Interagency Committee shall include representatives from the Department of Commerce (including the National Oceanic and Atmospheric Administration and the

National Institute of Standards and Technology), the Department of Energy, the Department of the Interior (including the Minerals Management Service and the United States Fish and Wildlife Service), the Department of Transportation (including the United States Coast Guard, the Maritime Administration, and the Research and Special Projects Administration), the Department of Defense (including the Army Corps of Engineers and the Navy), the Environmental Protection Agency, the National Aeronautics and Space Administration, and the United States Fire Administration in the Federal Emergency Management Agency, as well as such other Federal agencies as the President may designate.

A representative of the Department of Transportation shall serve as Chairman.

    (b) OIL POLLUTION RESEARCH AND TECHNOLOGY PLAN.—

        (1) IMPLEMENTATION PLAN.—Within 180 days after the date of enactment of this Act, the Interagency Committee shall submit to Congress a plan for the implementation of the oil pollution research, development, and demonstration program established pursuant to subsection (c). The research plan shall—

            (A) identify agency roles and responsibilities;

            (B) assess the current status of knowledge on oil pollution prevention, response, and mitigation technologies and effects of oil pollution on the environment;

            (C) identify significant oil pollution research gaps including an assessment of major technological deficiencies in responses to past oil discharges;

            (D) establish research priorities and goals for oil pollution technology development related to prevention, response, mitigation, and environmental effects;

            (E) estimate the resources needed to conduct the oil pollution research and development program established pursuant to subsection (c), and timetables for completing research tasks; and

            (F) identify, in consultation with the States, regional oil pollution research needs and priorities for a coordinated, multidisciplinary program of research at the regional level.

        (2) ADVICE AND GUIDANCE.—The Chairman, through the Department of Transportation, shall contract with the National Academy of Sciences to—

            (A) provide advice and guidance in the preparation and development of the research plan; and

            (B) assess the adequacy of the plan as submitted, and submit a report to Congress on the conclusions of such assessment.

The National Institute of Standards and Technology shall provide the Interagency Committee with advice and guidance on issues relating to quality assurance and standards measurements relating to its activities under this section.

    (c) OIL POLLUTION RESEARCH AND DEVELOPMENT PROGRAM.—

        (1) ESTABLISHMENT.—The Interagency Committee shall coordinate the establishment, by the agencies represented on the Interagency Committee, of a program for conducting oil pollution research and development, as provided in this subsection.

December 29, 2000

154

(2) INNOVATIVE OIL POLLUTION TECHNOLOGY.—The program established under this subsection shall provide for research, development, and demonstration of new or improved technologies which are effective in preventing or mitigating oil discharges and which protect the environment, including—

(A) development of improved designs for vessels and facilities, and improved operational practices;

(B) research, development, and demonstration of improved technologies to measure the ullage of a vessel tank, prevent discharges from tank vents, prevent discharges during lightering and bunkering operations, contain discharges on the deck of a vessel, prevent discharges through the use of vacuums in tanks, and otherwise contain discharges of oil from vessels and facilities;

(C) research, development, and demonstration of new or improved systems of mechanical, chemical, biological, and other methods (including the use of dispersants, solvents, and bioremediation) for the recovery, removal, and disposal of oil, including evaluation of the environmental effects of the use of such systems;

(D) research and training, in consultation with the National Response Team, to improve industry's and Government's ability to quickly and effectively remove an oil discharge, including the long-term use, as appropriate, of the National Spill Control School in Corpus Christi, Texas, and the Center for Marine Training and Safety in Galveston, Texas;

(E) research to improve information systems for decisionmaking, including the use of data from coastal mapping, baseline data, and other data related to the environmental effects of oil discharges, and cleanup technologies;

(F) development of technologies and methods to protect public health and safety from oil discharges, including the population directly exposed to an oil discharge;

(G) development of technologies, methods, and standards for protecting removal personnel, including training, adequate supervision, protective equipment, maximum exposure limits, and decontamination procedures;

(H) research and development of methods to restore and rehabilitate natural resources damaged by oil discharges;

(I) research to evaluate the relative effectiveness and environmental impacts of bioremediation technologies; and

(J) the demonstration of a satellite-based, dependent surveillance vessel traffic system in Narragansett Bay to evaluate the utility of such system in reducing the risk of oil discharges from vessel collisions and groundings in confined waters.

(3) OIL POLLUTION TECHNOLOGY EVALUATION.—The program established under this subsection shall provide for oil pollution prevention and mitigation technology evaluation including—

(A) the evaluation and testing of technologies developed independently of the research and development program established under this subsection;

(B) the establishment, where appropriate, of standards and testing protocols traceable to national standards to measure the performance of oil pollution prevention or mitigation technologies; and

(C) the use, where appropriate, of controlled field testing to evaluate real-world application of oil discharge prevention or mitigation technologies.

(4) OIL POLLUTION EFFECTS RESEARCH.—(A) The Committee shall establish a research program to monitor and evaluate the environmental effects of oil discharges. Such program shall include the following elements:

(i) The development of improved models and capabilities for predicting the environmental fate, transport, and effects of oil discharges.

(ii) The development of methods, including economic methods, to assess damages to natural resources resulting from oil discharges.

(iii) The identification of types of ecologically sensitive areas at particular risk to oil discharges and the preparation of scientific monitoring and evaluation plans, one for each of several types of ecological conditions, to be implemented in the event of major oil discharges in such areas.

(iv) The collection of environmental baseline data in ecologically sensitive areas at particular risk to oil discharges where such data are insufficient.

(B) The Department of Commerce in consultation with the Environmental Protection Agency shall monitor and scientifically evaluate the long-term environmental effects of oil discharges if—

(i) the amount of oil discharged exceeds 250,000 gallons;

(ii) the oil discharge has occurred on or after January 1, 1989; and

(iii) the Interagency Committee determines that a study of the long-term environmental effects of the discharge would be of significant scientific value, especially for preventing or responding to future oil discharges.

Areas for study may include the following sites where oil discharges have occurred: the New York/New Jersey Harbor area, where oil was discharged by an Exxon underwater pipeline, the T/B CIBRO SAVANNAH, and the M/V BT NAUTILUS; Narragansett Bay where oil was discharged by the WORLD PRODIGY; the Houston Ship Channel where oil was discharged by the RACHEL B; the Delaware River, where oil was discharged by the PRESIDENTE RIVERA, and Huntington Beach, California, where oil was discharged by the AMERICAN TRADER.

(C) Research conducted under this paragraph by, or through, the United States Fish and Wildlife Service shall be directed and coordinated by the National Wetland Research Center.

(5) MARINE SIMULATION RESEARCH.—The program established under this subsection shall include research on the greater use and application of geographic and vessel response simulation models, including the development of additional data bases and updating of existing data bases using, among

DOCUMENT 3

House of Representatives, Committee on Merchant Marine and Fisheries, Subcommittee on Coast Guard and Navigation, February 17, March 18, 1993. Hearing on the Oil Pollution Act of 1990 and its role in reducing oil spills and assuring response capability.
Front page, Committee's and Subcommittee's Components, Contents.

THE OIL POLLUTION ACT OF 1990

HEARING

BEFORE THE

SUBCOMMITTEE ON
COAST GUARD AND NAVIGATION

OF THE

COMMITTEE ON
MERCHANT MARINE AND FISHERIES
HOUSE OF REPRESENTATIVES

ONE HUNDRED THIRD CONGRESS

FIRST SESSION

ON

THE OIL POLLUTION ACT OF 1990 AND ITS ROLE IN RE-DUCING OIL SPILLS AND ASSURING RESPONSE CAPA-BILITY

FEBRUARY 17, MARCH 18, 1993

Serial No. 103–8

Printed for the use of the Committee on Merchant Marine and Fisheries

U.S. GOVERNMENT PRINTING OFFICE

68–199 ≊   WASHINGTON : 1993

For sale by the U.S. Government Printing Office
Superintendent of Documents, Congressional Sales Office, Washington, DC 20402
ISBN 0-16-041040-1

159

COMMITTEE ON MERCHANT MARINE AND FISHERIES

GERRY E. STUDDS, Massachusetts, *Chairman*

WILLIAM J. HUGHES, New Jersey
EARL HUTTO, Florida
W.J. (BILLY) TAUZIN, Louisiana
WILLIAM O. LIPINSKI, Illinois
SOLOMON P. ORTIZ, Texas
THOMAS J. MANTON, New York
OWEN B. PICKETT, Virginia
GEORGE J. HOCHBRUECKNER, New York
FRANK PALLONE, JR., New Jersey
GREG LAUGHLIN, Texas
JOLENE UNSOELD, Washington
GENE TAYLOR, Mississippi
JACK REED, Rhode Island
H. MARTIN LANCASTER, North Carolina
THOMAS H. ANDREWS, Maine
ELIZABETH FURSE, Oregon
LYNN SCHENK, California
GENE GREEN, Texas
ALCEE L. HASTINGS, Florida
DAN HAMBURG, California
BLANCHE M. LAMBERT, Arkansas
ANNA G. ESHOO, California
THOMAS J. BARLOW, III, Kentucky
BART STUPAK, Michigan
MARIA CANTWELL, Washington
PETER DEUTSCH, Florida
GARY L. ACKERMAN, New York

JACK FIELDS, Texas
DON YOUNG, Alaska
HERBERT H. BATEMAN, Virginia
JIM SAXTON, New Jersey
HOWARD COBLE, North Carolina
CURT WELDON, Pennsylvania
JAMES M. INHOFE, Oklahoma
ARTHUR RAVENEL, JR., South Carolina
WAYNE T. GILCHREST, Maryland
RANDY "DUKE" CUNNINGHAM, California
JACK KINGSTON, Georgia
TILLIE K. FOWLER, Florida
MICHAEL N. CASTLE, Delaware
PETER T. KING, New York
LINCOLN DIAZ-BALART, Florida
RICHARD W. POMBO, California

JEFFREY R. PIKE, *Staff Director*
WILLIAM W. STELLE, JR., *Chief Counsel*
MARY J. FUSCO KITSOS, *Chief Clerk*
HARRY F. BURROUGHS, *Minority Staff Director*

SUBCOMMITTEE ON COAST GUARD AND NAVIGATION

W.J. (BILLY) TAUZIN, Louisiana, *Chairman*

WILLIAM J. HUGHES, New Jersey
EARL HUTTO, Florida
H. MARTIN LANCASTER, North Carolina
THOMAS J. BARLOW III, Kentucky
BART STUPAK, Michigan
WILLIAM O. LIPINSKI, Illinois
OWEN B. PICKETT, Virginia
GEORGE J. HOCHBRUECKNER, New York
FRANK PALLONE, JR., New Jersey
GREG LAUGHLIN, Texas
LYNN SCHENK, California
ALCEE L. HASTINGS, Florida
BLANCHE M. LAMBERT, Arkansas
GENE TAYLOR, Mississippi
GERRY E. STUDDS, Massachusetts
  (Ex Officio)

HOWARD COBLE, North Carolina
HERBERT H. BATEMAN, Virginia
WAYNE T. GILCHREST, Maryland
TILLIE K. FOWLER, Florida
MICHAEL N. CASTLE, Delaware
PETER T. KING, New York
LINCOLN DIAZ-BALART, Florida
JAMES M. INHOFE, Oklahoma
JACK FIELDS, Texas (Ex Officio)

ELIZABETH MEGGINSON, *Staff Director/Counsel*
JAMES L. ADAMS, *Professional Staff*
ED LEE, *Minority Professional Staff*

(II)

CONTENTS

(III)

161

IV

DOCUMENT 4

WRITTEN TESTIMONY OF ENDTECH INC. TO THE HOUSE
SUBCOMMITTEE ON COAST GUARD AND NAVIGATION
(Prepared with the assistance of David W. Burgett, James D.
Freeman, Hogan & Hartson)

WRITTEN TESTIMONY OF ENDTECH, INC.

TO THE HOUSE SUBCOMMITTEE ON
COAST GUARD AND NAVIGATION

HEARING ON THE IMPLEMENTATION OF
SECTION 4202(a)(6) OF THE OIL POLLUTION ACT OF 1990
REQUIRING OIL-CARRYING VESSELS
TO CARRY DISCHARGE RESPONSE EQUIPMENT

March 31, 1993   Prepared with the
                                        assistance of:

                                        David W. Burgett
                                        James D. Freeman
                                        Hogan & Hartson

Endtech, Inc. appreciates this opportunity to present its views on the Coast Guard's implementation of Section 4202(a)(6) of the Oil Pollution Act of 1990 ("Oil Pollution Act" or "the Act"). Endtech designs oil skimming equipment and vessels that, unlike other currently available skimmers, are capable of being operated in open seas under less-than-ideal conditions. Key aspects of Endtech's skimmer designs have already been tested by official bodies of certification such as Lloyd's Register of Shipping and the Italian National Institute for Naval Architecture Studies and Experiences. Further testing of the full design and oil conveying apparatus, as well as the skimming mechanism itself, is planned to be conducted at the U.S. Navy's David Taylor Research Center later this year. Endtech has patent applications pending for its vessels and towed skimming systems in both the United States and Europe and has already sold other skimmers in Europe.

Endtech is interested in ensuring that the regulations promulgated under the Oil Pollution Act fulfill the Act's directive requiring vessels operating in the navigable waters of the United States and carrying oil in bulk as cargo to carry discharge removal equipment on board that reflects the best technology economically feasible. Since most cleanup activities are likely to be conducted from vessels that do not carry oil, Endtech also is interested in ensuring that the Coast Guard implements the congressional purpose reflected in the Oil Pollution Act by requiring the oil shipping industry to use recovery vessels that carry the best cleanup technology

economically feasible when the agency reviews and approves Vessel
Response Plans and National and Area Contingency Plans pursuant
to 33 U.S.C. §§ 1321(j)(5), 1321(d) and 1321(j)(4).

I.   CONGRESSIONAL INTENT IN ENACTING THE OIL POLLUTION
        CONTROL ACT

        Congress enacted the Oil Pollution Act in response to four
major oil spills near coastal areas of the United States in the
late 1980s. See S. Rep. No. 94, 101st Cong., 2d Sess. 2 (1990),
reprinted in 1990 U.S.C.C.A.N. 722, 723-24. Each of these oil
spills severely damaged the surrounding marine environment. The
largest and most publicized of the spills, the Exxon Valdez
disaster, released eleven million gallons of oil into Prince
William Sound, Alaska. Id. Congress noted that the disaster
"was exacerbated greatly by the unreasonably slow, confused and
inadequate response by industry and government that failed
miserably in containing the spill and preventing damage." Id.

        The Oil Pollution Act contains several provisions designed
to ensure the adequacy of future response actions.
Section 4202(a)(6), the subject of this hearing, requires the
President to promulgate regulations requiring "vessels operating
on navigable waters and carrying oil or a hazardous substance in
bulk as cargo to carry appropriate removal equipment that employs
the best technology economically feasible and that is compatible
with the safe operation of the vessel." 33 U.S.C.
§ 1321(j)(6)(B). Congress certainly envisioned that the

- 2 -

167

technology considered and eventually required would assist government and industry disaster relief workers in their efforts to contain future oil spills of a magnitude comparable to the Exxon Valdez disaster.

The language of the statute reflects the congressional desire to set standards for removal equipment for on-water containment and removal of oil spills. The terms "remove or removal" are defined as the "containment and removal of the oil or hazardous substances from the water and shorelines or the taking of such other actions as may be necessary to minimize or mitigate damage to the public health or welfare . . . ." 33 U.S.C. § 1321(a)(8) (emphasis supplied). Thus, the language of the statute does not limit discharge removal equipment to on-deck removal; in fact, its focus is on on-water removal of oil. There is thus no doubt that Congress intended the "best technology economically feasible" standard to be applied to on-water oil removal equipment.

II.   THE COAST GUARD'S PROPOSED RULE

Despite this clear congressional intent, the proposed rule issued by the Coast Guard does not require any technology, much less the best technology, for the removal of discharges into the water. See 57 Fed. Reg. 44,912, 44,915 (Sept. 29, 1992). Instead, the proposed regulation focuses on on-deck discharges. For example, vessels greater than 400 feet in length need only

carry discharge removal equipment that is capable of removing
on-deck spills of up to twelve barrels under the proposed rule.
Id. at 44,919. While the containment and removal of on-deck oil
spills is certainly deserving of attention, such spills are
trivial in comparison to the large on-water oil spills that
Congress was concerned about in enacting the Oil Pollution Act.

According to the preamble to the proposed rule, the
Coast Guard did not require vessels to warehouse on-water
containment and removal equipment because the primary
responsibilities of a vessel's crew are the safety of the vessel
and the containment of the cargo. Id. at 44,915. The Coast
Guard also claims that deployment of crew members in on-water
removal action may jeopardize their safety and the safe operation
of the vessel. Id. As an alternative to requiring the
warehousing of on-water removal equipment, the negotiated
rulemaking committee "agreed to set on-scene planning criteria
for on-water containment and removal of spilled oil. Vessel
owners or operators could meet these planning criteria with
carried equipment or rapid mobilization of shore-based
equipment." Id. In other words, the Coast Guard proposes to
give operators flexibility in determining where to base the
necessary technology, subject to the contingency plan approval
process.

In considering the feasibility and effectiveness of
on-board equipment, one needs to distinguish containment from

- 4 -

169

removal systems. It may be that containment devices can play a role in reducing the spread of an oil slick pending the arrival of shore-based equipment.

Skimming equipment is another story. Endtech agrees that on-water removal should not compromise crew-member safety or the safe operation of vessels carrying oil. Moreover, specially-designed and equipped shore-based recovery vessels will often be more effective than tanker-based systems. Use of shore-based recovery vessels would permit a more flexible response, with vessels capable of operating under a wide range of working conditions, including water depth, sea bottom configuration, and the magnitude of the oil spill. The vessels will also provide response teams with the capability to transport some "first intervention" equipment by air cargo. For these reasons, Endtech believes that the most effective spill response strategy would integrate use of shore-based recovery vessels and on-board containment equipment. However, if such flexibility is to be accorded, it is absolutely critical that the Coast Guard require operators to utilize the best technology feasible for shore-based removal equipment. Otherwise, operators would be able to avoid utilizing the best technology by opting to use only shore-based systems. Such a result would contravene the congressional purpose in enacting the Oil Pollution Act. Therefore, the Coast Guard must apply the "best technology economically feasible" standard to shore-based technology proposed in vessel response and contingency plans.

170

This would be perfectly consistent with the Act's provisions on review of plans. Requiring vessel response plans and area contingency plans to call for the use of removal equipment that utilize the best technology economically feasible is consistent with the provisions of the Act mandating these plans. Section 4202(a)(6) requires area contingency plans to "list the equipment . . . available to an owner or operator and Federal, State, and local agencies, to ensure an effective and immediate removal of a discharge . . . ." 33 U.S.C. § 1321(j)(4)(C)(iv) (emphasis supplied). The same section of the Act also requires vessel owners to submit response plans that "identify . . . private personnel and equipment necessary to remove to the maximum extent practicable a worst case discharge . . . ." Id. § 1321(j)(5)(C)(iii) (emphasis supplied). Thus, both provisions contain independent requirements for utilization of the most effective removal equipment technology possible. The Coast Guard must ensure that this congressional mandate is reflected in its regulations.

III. THE COAST GUARD MUST DEVELOP OBJECTIVE STANDARDS FOR COMPARING OIL SPILL REMOVAL TECHNOLOGIES.

The Oil Pollution Act also displays a clear congressional intent to establish objective standards for the evaluation of oil spill removal technologies. For example, Section 7001(b)(2) of the Act states: "The National Institute of Standards and Technology shall provide the Interagency Committee

with advice and guidance on issues relating to quality assurance
and standards measurements relating to its activities under this
section." 33 U.S.C. § 2761(b)(2). In addition, Section
7001(c)(3) requires the establishment of "standards and testing
protocols traceable to national standards to measure the
performance of oil pollution prevention or mitigation
technologies . . . ." Id. § 2761(c)(3).

Neither the Interagency Committee nor the Coast Guard
has established the objective standards for determining the best
technology envisioned in the Oil Pollution Act. The Coast
Guard's failure to establish objective standards in its proposed
rule creates several serious problems. Most importantly, vessel
owners and oil spill response authorities will be unable to make
sound, objective decisions when choosing between competing
technologies. If vessel owners and oil spill response
authorities unknowingly purchase less effective equipment, it
will diminish their ability to respond to oil spills.

The introduction of objective standards also would
create market-based incentives to improve discharge removal
technologies. When faced with competing technologies, the oil
transport industry would be more likely to purchase equipment
that has been determined to be the most effective in real-world
conditions. This would create a corresponding incentive for the
discharge removal industry to develop new removal systems and
improve existing equipment.

Finally, the existence of objective standards would enable a more honest valuation of oil spill response capabilities. As the Coast Guard's proposed and interim final regulations implementing the Oil Pollution Act now stand, skimmer effectiveness may be measured by the removal capacity stated on the skimmer's nameplate. However, the nameplate capacity is not based on actual test results under realistic conditions, but on theoretical maximum throughput, which is likely to overstate real performance by many times. Thus, the removal capacity listed on skimmer nameplates does not reflect skimmers' true capabilities. The misleading removal capacity information on skimmer nameplates has two consequences. First, vessel owners and other spill response authorities have much smaller true response capacities than reliance on nameplate capacity would indicate. Second, vessel owners and other spill response authorities cannot easily determine whether one type of removal equipment will be more successful at removing spilled oil under real-world conditions than another. These shortcomings are not cured by the application of an arbitrary "efficiency factor" of 20%, as provided for in the related vessel response plan interim final rules. See 58 Fed. Reg. 7376, 7413, 7442 (Feb. 5, 1993). Multiplication of a meaningless and unreliable number by this factor simply results in another meaningless figure and fails utterly to distinguish technology that is effective under real conditions from that which is not.

- 8 -

Accordingly, the Coast Guard's failure to establish objective standards to measure discharge removal capability acts as a disincentive to the development of more efficient removal technology. To ensure that oil spill recovery efforts achieve the most effective response possible, the Coast Guard should establish objective test standards and require vessel response plans and area contingency plans to use the on-water removal equipment that achieves the best test results. Only then would the Coast Guard meet the congressional objectives of the Oil Pollution Act.

The Coast Guard can establish objective standards for determining the effectiveness of discharge removal technology relatively easily. The American Society for Testing and Materials ("ASTM") has developed performance standards for skimmer equipment, including the Standard Test Method for Full Scale Advancing Spill Removal Devices (Standard No. F631-80) and the Standard Guide for Collecting Skimmer Performance Data in Uncontrolled Environments (Standard No. F808-83). ASTM is currently revising these standards to reflect industry capabilities more accurately. Moreover, skimmer technology may be evaluated at the Oil and Hazardous Materials Simulated Test Tank ("OHMSETT") Research Center, the David Taylor Research Center, or other test tank facilities to determine comparative performance levels applying OHMSETT and ASTM standards. Accordingly, the Coast Guard may look to objective performance standards already developed by the private sector.

- 9 -

174

It is our hope that the Subcommittee will address in future hearings and, if necessary, legislation, the need for planning based on objective performance standards and mandatory testing of all devices used to meet Oil Pollution Act requirements.

Thank you for considering this testimony.

1825F

DOCUMENT 5

Burgett David W. (Hogan & Hartson): Endtech comments to the Executive Secretary, Marine Safety Council, in response to the Coast Guard's proposed rule regarding Discharge Removal Equipment for Vessels Carrying Oil.

213

HOGAN & HARTSON

COLUMBIA SQUARE
555 THIRTEENTH STREET NW
WASHINGTON DC 20004-1109
(202) 637-5600

BRUSSELS
LONDON
PARIS
PRAGUE
WARSAW
BALTIMORE MD
BETHESDA MD
McLEAN VA

DAVID W. BURGETT
PARTNER
DIRECT DIAL (202) 637-6407

November 16, 1992

BY HAND

Executive Secretary
Marine Safety Council
U.S. Coast Guard Headquarters
Room 3406
2100 Second Street, SW
Washington, DC 20593-0001

Re: CGD 90-068

Dear Sir or Madam:

These comments are submitted on behalf of Endtech, Inc.
in response to the Coast Guard's proposed rule regarding
Discharge Removal Equipment for Vessels Carrying Oil. See 57
Fed. Reg. 44,912 (Sept. 29, 1992).

INTEREST OF ENDTECH

Endtech designs oil skimming equipment and vessels that,
unlike other currently available skimmers, truly are capable of
being operated in open seas. Some of its designs have already
been tested by official bodies of certification such as Lloyd's
Register of Shipping and the Italian National Institute for Naval
Architecture Studies and Experiences and put into service in
Europe. Endtech has patent applications pending for this
equipment in both the United States and Europe. Thus, Endtech is
interested in ensuring that the regulations promulgated under the
Oil Pollution Act of 1990 ("Oil Pollution Act" or "the Act")
fulfill the Act's directive that requires vessels operating in
the navigable waters of the United States and carrying oil in
bulk as cargo to carry discharge removal equipment on board that
reflects the best technology economically feasible. Since most
cleanup activities are likely to be conducted from vessels that
do not carry oil, Endtech is also interested in ensuring that the
Coast Guard implements the congressional purpose reflected in the
Oil Pollution Act by requiring the oil shipping industry to use
recovery vessels that carry the best cleanup technology

FAX (202) 637-5910 TELEX 8485 (HOGAL 89775) (WU) CABLE: HOGANDER WASHINGTON

179

HOGAN & HARTSON

economically feasible when the agency reviews and approves Vessel Response Plans and National and Area Contingency Plans pursuant to 33 U.S.C. §§ 1321(j)(5), 1321(d) and 1321(j)(4).

CONGRESSIONAL INTENT IN ENACTING THE OIL POLLUTION CONTROL ACT

Congress enacted the Oil Pollution Act in response to four major oil spills near coastal areas of the United States in the late 1980s. See S. Rep. No. 94, 101st Cong., 2d Sess. 2 (1990), reprinted in 1990 U.S.C.C.A.N. 722, 723-24. Each of these oil spills severely damaged the surrounding marine environment. The largest and most publicized of the spills, the Exxon Valdez disaster, released eleven million gallons of oil into Prince William Sound, Alaska. Id. Congress noted that the disaster "was exacerbated greatly by the unreasonably slow, confused and inadequate response by industry and government that failed miserably in containing the spill and preventing damage." Id.

The Oil Pollution Act contains several provisions designed to ensure the adequacy of future response actions. One important provision, Section 4202(a)(6), requires the President to promulgate regulations requiring "vessels operating on navigable waters and carrying oil or a hazardous substance in bulk as cargo to carry appropriate removal equipment that employs the best technology economically feasible and that is compatible with the safe operation of the vessel." 33 U.S.C. § 1321(j)(6)(B). Congress certainly envisioned that the technology considered and eventually required would assist government and industry disaster relief workers in their efforts to contain future oil spills of a magnitude comparable to the Exxon Valdez disaster.

The language of the statute reflects the congressional desire to set standards for removal equipment for on-water containment and removal of oil spills. The terms "remove or removal" are defined as the "containment and removal of the oil or hazardous substances from the water and shorelines or the taking of such other actions as may be necessary to minimize or mitigate damage to the public health or welfare . . . ." 33 U.S.C. § 1321(a)(8) (emphasis supplied). Thus, the language of the statute does not limit discharge removal equipment to on-deck removal; in fact, its focus is on on-water removal of

215

HOGAN & HARTSON

Executive Secretary
Marine Safety Council
November 16, 1992
Page 3

oil. There is thus no doubt that Congress intended the "best
technology economically feasible" standard to be applied to
on-water oil removal equipment.

THE PROPOSED RULE

However, the proposed regulation focuses on on-deck
discharges. It does not require any technology, much less the
best technology, for the removal of discharges into the water.
While the containment and removal of on-deck oil spills is
certainly deserving of attention, such spills are trivial in
comparison to the large on-water oil spills that Congress was
concerned about in enacting the Oil Pollution Act. */

According to the preamble to the proposed rule, the
Coast Guard did not require vessels to warehouse on-water
containment and removal equipment because the primary
responsibilities of a vessel's crew are the safety of the vessel
and the containment of the cargo. Id. at 44,915. Moreover,
deployment of crew members in on-water removal action may
jeopardize their safety and the safe operation of the vessel.
Id. As an alternative to requiring the warehousing of on-water
removal equipment, the negotiated rulemaking committee "agreed to
set on-scene planning criteria for on-water containment and
removal of spilled oil. Vessel owners or operators could meet
these planning criteria with carried equipment or rapid
mobilization of shore-based equipment." Id. In other words, the
Coast Guard proposes to give operators flexibility in determining
where to base the necessary technology, subject to the
contingency plan approval process.

Endtech agrees that on-water removal should not
compromise crew-member safety or the safe operation of the
vessel. Moreover, specially-designed and equipped shore-based

---

*/ For example, discharge removal equipment for on-deck spills
for vessels greater than 400 feet in length need only be capable
of removing spills of up to twelve barrels. 57 Fed. Reg. at
44,919.

HOGAN & HARTSON

recovery vessels will often be more effective than tanker-based systems. Use of shore-based recovery vessels would permit a more flexible response, with vessels capable of operating under a wide range of working conditions, including water depth, sea bottom configuration, and the magnitude of the oil spill. The vessels will also provide response teams with the capability to transport some "first intervention" equipment by air cargo. For these reasons, Endtech does not disagree in principle with the concept of using the best feasible shore-based systems as an alternative to warehousing on-water removal equipment aboard vessels that carry oil. However, if such flexibility is to be accorded, it is absolutely critical that the Coast Guard require operators to utilize the best technology feasible for shore-based removal equipment. Otherwise, operators would be able to avoid utilizing the best technology by opting to use only shore-based systems. Such a result would contravene the congressional purpose in enacting the Oil Pollution Act. Therefore, the Coast Guard must apply the "best technology economically feasible" standard to shore-based technology proposed in vessel response and contingency plans.

This would be perfectly consistent with the Act's provisions on review of plans. Requiring vessel response plans and area contingency plans to call for the use of removal equipment that utilize the best technology economically feasible is consistent with the provisions of the Act mandating these plans. Section 4202(a)(6) requires area contingency plans to "list the equipment . . . available to an owner or operator and Federal, State, and local agencies, to ensure an effective and immediate removal of a discharge . . . ." 33 U.S.C. § 1321(j)(4)(C)(iv) (emphasis supplied). The same section of the Act also requires vessel owners to submit response plans that "identify . . . private personnel and equipment necessary to remove to the maximum extent practicable a worst case discharge . . . ." Id. § 1321(j)(5)(C)(iii) (emphasis supplied). Thus, both provisions contain independent requirements for utilization of the most effective removal equipment technology possible. The Coast Guard must ensure that this congressional mandate is reflected in its regulations.

The Oil Pollution Act also displays a clear congressional intent to develop objective standards for developing innovative technologies for oil pollution prevention and to establish objective standards for the evaluation of such technologies. For example, Section 7001(b)(2) of the Act

HOGAN & HARTSON

states: "The National Institute of Standards and Technology shall provide the Interagency Committee with advice and guidance on issues relating to quality assurance and standards measurements relating to its activities under this section." 33 U.S.C. § 2761(b)(2). In addition, Section 7001(c)(3) requires the establishment of "standards and testing protocols traceable to national standards to measure the performance of oil pollution prevention or mitigation technologies . . . ." Id. § 2761(c)(3).

While the Interagency Committee has not yet endorsed standards as envisioned in the Oil Pollution Act, industry has established national standards by which the Coast Guard can determine what discharge removal technology is most effective. The American Society for Testing and Materials ("ASTM") has developed performance standards for skimmer equipment, including the Standard Test Method for Full Scale Advancing Spill Removal Devices (F631-80) and the Standard Guide for Collecting Skimmer Performance Data in Uncontrolled Environments (F808-83). ASTM is currently revising these standards to reflect industry capabilities more accurately. Skimmer technology may be evaluated at the Oil and Hazardous Materials Simulated Test Tank ("OHMSETT") Research Center to determine comparative performance levels applying OHMSETT and ASTM standards. To ensure that oil spill recovery efforts achieve the most effective response possible, the Coast Guard should require vessel response plans and area contingency plans to utilize the on-water removal equipment that achieves the best test results under these objective standards. The Coast Guard can only meet the congressional objectives of the Oil Pollution Act by requiring the use of the best on-water discharge removal equipment as recognized by the application of objective national standards.

Thank you for considering these comments. Please contact the undersigned if we can provide any further information.

Sincerely,

David W. Burgett

1305F

DOCUMENT 6

DEPARTMENT OF TRANSPORTATION
Coast Guard
33 CFR Part 155
(CGD 91-034)
RIN 2115-AD81
Vessel Response Plans
AGENCY: Coast Guard, DOT.
ACTION: Notice of proposed rulemaking.
Federal Register / Vol. 57, No 119 / Friday, June 19, 1992 / pages
27550 and 27551 / points 6.2.1. and 6.2.2. (Nameplate Formula)

average temperature ranges expected in a geographic area in which a vessel operates. All equipment identified in a response plan must be designed to operate within those conditions or ranges.

2.6 The requirements of subpart D of this part establish response resource mobilization and response times. The location that the vessel operates farthest from the storage location of the response resource must be used to determine whether the resources can arrive on scene within the time required. A vessel owner or operator shall include the time for notification, mobilization, and travel time of resources identified to meet the maximum most probable discharge and Tier 1 worst case discharge requirements. Tier 2 and 3 resources must be notified and mobilized as necessary to meet the requirements for arrival on scene. An on water speed of 10 knots and a land speed of 35 miles per hour is assumed unless the vessel owner or operator can demonstrate otherwise.

2.7 In identifying equipment, the vessel owner or operator shall list the storage location, quantity, and manufacturer's make and model. For oil recovery devices, the effective daily recovery rate, as determined using section 6 of this appendix, must be included. For boom, the overall boom height must be included. A vessel owner or operator is responsible for ensuring that identified boom has compatible connectors.

3. Determining Response Resources Required for the Average Most Probable Discharge

3.1 A vessel owner or operator shall ensure that sufficient response resources are available to respond to the 50 barrel average most probable discharge. The equipment must be designed to function in the operating environment at the point of oil transfer.

3.1.1 These resources must be located at or near the site of operational transfers involving vessels that carry oil in bulk as a primary cargo:

.1 Containment boom in a quantity equal to twice the length of the largest vessel involved in the transfer and a means of immediate deployment.

.2 Oil recovery devices with an effective recovery rate of 50 barrel per day or greater available at the transfer site within two hours of the detection of an oil discharge.

.3 Oil storage capacity for recovered oily material indicated in section 9.2 of this appendix.

3.1.2 A vessel that carries oil in bulk as a secondary cargo must identify sources of equipment in its areas of operation. Deployment requirements in section 3.1.1 of this appendix need not be met for these vessels.

4. Determining Response Resources Required for the Maximum Most Probable Discharge

4.1 A vessel owner or operator shall ensure that sufficient response resources are available to respond to discharges up to the maximum most probable discharge volume for that vessel. This will require resources capable of containing and collecting up to 2,500 barrels of oil. All equipment identified must be designed to operate in the applicable operating environment specified in Table 1.

4.2 To determine the maximum most probable discharge volume to be used for planning, use the lesser of—

4.2.1 2500 barrels; or

4.2.2 10% of the total oil cargo capacity.

4.3 Oil recovery devices identified to meet the applicable maximum most probable discharge volume planning criteria must be located such that they arrive on scene within 12 hours in higher volume port areas and the Great Lakes and 24 hours in all other river, inland, nearshore, and offshore areas.

4.3.1 Because rapid control, containment, and removal of oil is critical to reduce spill impact, the effective daily recovery rate for oil recovery devices must equal 50% of the planning volume applicable for the vessel as determined in section 4.2 of this appendix. The effective daily recovery rate for oil recovery devices identified in the plan must be determined using the criteria in section 6 of this appendix.

4.4 In addition to oil recovery capacity, the plan must identify and ensure the availability of, through contract or other approved means, sufficient boom available within the required response times for oil collection and containment and for protection of shoreline areas. While the regulation does not set required quantities of boom, the response plan must identify and ensure the availability of the quantity of boom available through contract or other approved means.

4.5 The plan must indicate the availability of temporary storage capacity to meet the requirements of section 9.2 of this appendix. If available storage capacity is insufficient to meet this requirement, then the effective daily recovery rate must be derated to the limits of the available storage capacity.

4.6 The following is an example of a maximum most probable discharge volume planning calculation for equipment identification in a higher volume port area:

The vessel's capacity is 10,000 barrels, thus the planning volume is 10 percent or 1,000 barrels. The effective daily recovery rate must be 50% of this, or 500 barrels per day. The ability of oil recovery devices to meet this capacity will be calculated using the procedures in section 6 of this appendix. Temporary storage capacity available on scene must equal twice the daily recovery rate as indicated in section 9 of this appendix, or 1000 barrels per day. This is the information the vessel owner or operator would use to identify and ensure the availability of, through contract or other approved means, the required response resources. The vessel owner would also need to identify how much boom was available for use.

5. Determining Response Resources Required for the Worst Case Discharge to the Maximum Extent Practicable

5.1 A vessel owner or operator shall specify the availability of sufficient response resources to respond to the worst case discharge of oil cargo to the maximum extent practicable. Section 7 describes the method to determine the required response resources.

5.2 Oil spill recovery devices identified to meet the applicable worst case discharge planning volume must be located such that they can arrive at the scene of a discharge

within the time specified for the applicable response tier listed in § 155.1050.

5.3 The effective daily recovery rate for oil recovery devices identified in a response plan must be determined using the criteria in section 6 of this appendix. A vessel owner or operator shall identify the storage locations of all equipment that must be used to fulfill the requirements for each tier. The owner or operator of a vessel whose required daily recovery capacity exceeds the applicable contracting caps in Table 6 shall identify sources of additional equipment, their locations, and the arrangements made to obtain this equipment during a response. While general listings of available response equipment may be used to identify additional sources, a response plan must identify the specific sources and quantities of equipment that a vessel owner or operator has considered in their planning.

5.4 In addition to oil recovery devices, a vessel owner or operator shall identify and ensure the availability of, through contract or other approved means, sufficient boom that can arrive on scene within the required response times for oil containment and collection and for protection of shoreline areas. Table 2 lists the minimum quantities of boom for shoreline protection that a vessel owner or operator shall identify and ensure the availability of, through contract or other approved means.

5.5 A vessel owner or operator shall identify the availability of temporary storage capacity to meet the requirements of section 9.2 of this appendix. If available storage capacity is insufficient to meet this requirement, then the effective daily recovery rate must be derated to the limits of the available storage capacity.

6. Determining Effective Daily Recovery Rate for Oil Recovery Devices

6.1 Oil recovery devices identified by a vessel owner or operator must be identified by manufacturer, model, and effective daily recovery rate. These rates must be used to determine whether there is sufficient capacity to meet the applicable planning criteria for the average most probable discharge; maximum most probable discharge; and worst case discharge to the maximum extent practicable.

6.2 For the purposes of determining the effective daily recovery rate of oil recovery devices, the following method will be used. This method considers potential limitations due to available daylight, weather, sea state, and percentage of emulsified oil in the recovered material. The Coast Guard may assign a lower efficiency factor to equipment listed in a response plan if it determines that such a reduction is warranted.

6.2.1 The following formula must be used to calculate the effective daily recovery rate:
$R = T \times 24 \text{ hours} \times E$

R—Effective daily recovery rate

T—Throughput rate in barrels per hour (nameplate capacity)

E—20% Efficiency factor (or lower factor as determined by Coast Guard)

6.2.2 For those devices in which the pump limits the throughput of liquid, throughput

rate will be calculated using the pump capacity.

6.2.2 For belt or mop type devices, the throughput rate will be calculated using the speed of the belt or mop, surface area of the belt or mop in contact with the water surface; and the oil encounter rate. For purposes of this calculation, the assumed thickness of oil will be 1/4 inch.

6.3 As an alternative to 6.2, a vessel owner or operator may submit adequate evidence that a different effective daily recovery rate should be applied for a specific oil recovery device. Adequate evidence is actual verified performance data in spill conditions or tests using ASTM Standard F 631-80, F 808-83 (1988), or an equivalent test approved by the Coast Guard.

6.3.1 The following formula must be used to calculate the effective daily recovery rate under this alternative:

R = D × U

R—Effective daily recovery rate
D—Average Oil Recovery Rate in barrels per hour (Item 24 in F 808-83; Item 13.1.15 in F 631-80; or actual performance data)
U—Hours per day that a vessel owner or operator can document capability to operate equipment under spill conditions. Ten hours per day must be used unless a vessel owner or operator can demonstrate that the recovery operation can be sustained for longer periods.

6.4 A vessel owner or operator submitting a response plan shall provide data that supports the effective daily recovery rates for the oil recovery devices listed. The following is an example of these calculations:

A weir skimmer identified in a response plan has a manufacturer's rated throughput at the pump of 207 gallons per minute (gpm).
207 gpm = 301 barrels per hour
R = 301 × 24 × .2 = 1829 barrels per day

After testing using ASTM procedures, the skimmer's oil recovery rate is determined to be 220 gpm. The vessel owner or operator identifies sufficient resources available to support operations 12 hours per day.
220 gpm = 314 barrels per hour
R = 314 × 12 = 3768 barrels per day

A vessel owner or operator will be able to use the higher rate if sufficient temporary oil storage capacity is available.

7. Calculating the Worst Case Discharge Planning Volumes

7.1 A vessel owner or operator shall plan for a response to a vessel's worst case discharge volume of oil cargo. The planning for on-water recovery must take into account a loss of some oil to the environment due to evaporative and natural dissipation, potential increases in volume due to emulsification, and the potential for deposit of some oil on the shoreline.

7.2 The following procedures must be used to calculate the planning volume used by a vessel owner or operator for determining required on-water recovery capacity:

7.2.1 The following must be determined: the total volume of oil cargo carried, the appropriate cargo group for the type of oil carried (persistent [Groups 2, 3, 4] or nonpersistent [Group 1]), and the geographic area(s) in which the vessel operates. For vessels carrying mixed cargoes from different

oil groups, each group must be calculated separately. This information is to be used with Table 3 to determine the percentages of the total cargo volume to be used for removal capacity planning. This table divides the cargo volume into three categories: oil lost to the environment; oil deposited on the shoreline; and oil available for on-water recovery.

7.2.2 The on-water oil recovery volume must be adjusted using the appropriate emulsification factor found in Table 4.

7.2.3 The adjusted volume is multiplied by the on-water oil recovery resource mobilization factor found in Table 5 from the appropriate operating area and response tier to determine the total on water oil recovery capacity in barrels per day that must be identified or contracted for to arrive on-scene within the applicable time for each response tier. Three tiers are specified. For higher volume port areas and the Great Lakes, the contracted tiers of resources must be located such that they can arrive on-scene within 12, 36, and 60 hours of the discovery of an oil discharge. For all other river, inland, nearshore, and offshore areas, these tiers are 24, 48, and 72 hours. For the open ocean area, the tiers are 24, 48, and 72 hours with an additional travel time allowance of one hour for every additional 10 nautical miles beyond 50 miles from shore.

7.2.4 The resulting on-water recovery capacity in barrels per day for each tier is used to identify response resources necessary to sustain operations in the applicable geographic area. The equipment must be capable of sustaining operations for the time period specified in Table 3. A vessel owner or operator shall identify and ensure the availability of, through contract or other approved means, sufficient oil spill recovery devices to provide the effective daily oil recovery capacity required. If the required capacity exceeds the applicable cap specified in Table 5, then a vessel owner or operator shall contract only for the quantity of resources required to meet the cap, but shall identify sources of additional resources as indicated in section 6.3 of this appendix. The owner or operator of a vessel whose planning volume exceeds the cap to 1993 must make arrangements for additional capacity to be under contract by 1998 or 2003, as appropriate. For a vessel that carries multiple groups of oil, the required effective daily recovery capacity for each group is calculated before applying the cap.

7.3 The following procedures must be used to calculate the planning volume for identifying shoreline cleanup capacity:

7.3.1 The following must be determined: The total volume of oil cargo carried; the appropriate cargo group for the type of oil carried (persistent [Groups 2, 3, 4] or nonpersistent [Group 1]); and the geographic area(s) in which the vessel operates. For a vessel carrying cargoes from different oil groups, each group must be calculated separately. Using this information, Table 3 must be used to determine the percentages of the total cargo volume to be used for shoreline cleanup resource planning.

7.3.2 The shoreline cleanup planning volume must be adjusted to reflect an emulsification factor using the same procedure as described in section 7.2.2.

7.3.3 The resulting volume will be used to identify response resources necessary for shoreline cleanup.

7.4 The following is an example of the procedure described above:

A vessel with a 100,000 barrel capacity for #6 oil (specific gravity .96) will move from a higher volume port area to another area. The vessel's route will be 70 miles from shore.

Cargo carried: 100,000 bbls. Group 4 oil.
Emulsification factor: 1.9.
Areas transited: Inland, Nearshore, Offshore, Open ocean.
Planned % on-water recovery:
  Inland 50%
  Nearshore 50%
  Offshore 40%
  Open ocean 20%
Planned % oil onshore recovery:
  Inland 70%
  Nearshore 70%
  Offshore 30%
  Open ocean 30%
Planning volumes for on water recovery:
  Inland 100,000 × .5 × 1.8 = 90,000 bbls
  Nearshore 100,000 × .5 × 1.8 = 90,000 bbls
  Offshore 100,000 × .4 × 1.8 = 72,000 bbls
  Open ocean 100,000 × .2 × 1.8 = 36,000 bbls
Planning volumes for on shore recovery:
  Inland 100,000 × .7 × 1.8 = 126,000 bbls
  Nearshore 100,000 × .7 × 1.8 = 126,000 bbls
  Offshore 100,000 × .3 × 1.8 = 54,000 bbls
  Open ocean 100,000 × .3 × 1.8 = 54,000 bbls

The vessel owner or operator must contract with a response resource capable of managing a 126,000 barrel shoreline cleanup in those areas where the vessel comes closer than 50 miles to shore. There is no contract required for the 54,000 barrel capability required for open oceans if the vessel is operating farther than 50 miles from shore during the transit.

Determine required resources for on water recovery for each tier using mobilization factors:

	Tier 1	Tier 2	Tier 3
Inland/Nearshore			
90,000 ×	.15	.25	.40
Offshore 72,000 × .	.10	.16½	.21
Open ocean			
36,000 ×	.06	.10	.12
	equals (barrels per day)		
Inland/Nearshore ...	13,550	27,500	36,000
Offshore	7,200	11,880	15,120
Open ocean	2,160	3,600	4,320

Since the requirements for tiers 1 and 2 for inland and nearshore exceed the caps, the vessel owner would only need to contract for 10,000 bpd for tier 1 and 20,000 bpd for tier 2. Sources for the remaining 3,550 bpd for tier 1 and 2,500 for tier 2 would need to be identified but not contracted for.

The vessel owner or operator would also be required to identify or contract for quantities of boom identified in Table 2 for the areas that the vessel operates.

DOCUMENT 7-A

Letter: *Comments of the Marine Spill Response Corporation to the Notice of Proposed Rulemaking. CGD 91-034* sent on January 27, 1992 by the Marine Spill Response Corporation ("MSRC") to the Executive Secretary Marine Safety Council. And, from the attached documents: pages from 2 to 4 (out of a total of 22) of MSRC Supplementary Comments on Vessel Response Plan Issues.

Note the very telling warning engraved in capital letters, like a mantra by Rear Admiral John D. Costello on the lower side of the front page and on the attached tables: "INFORMATION PROVIDED HEREIN INVOLVES ASSUMPTIONS MADE SOLELY FOR PLANNING PURPOSES AND DOES NOT REFLECT PREDICTED ACTUAL PERFORMANCE IN ANY PARTICULAR SPILL EVENT. NOTHING IN THIS INFORMATIONISINTENDEDORSHOULDBEINTERPRETED AS A PROMISE OR STANDARD OF PERFORMANCE."

In short, NOTHING IN THIS INFORMATION IS INTENDED OR SHOULD BE INTERPRETED AS A PROMISE THAT WE WILL CLEAN UP ANY PARTICULAR SPILL EVENT.

MSRC 🌢
Marine Spill Response Corporation

JOHN D. COSTELLO
PRESIDENT

January 27, 1992

JAN 27 1991

Executive Secretary
Marine Safety Council
(G-LRA-2/3406)
(CGD 91-034/CGD 90-068)
U.S. Coast Guard Headquarters
2100 Second Street, S.W.
Washington, D.C. 20593-0001

    Re: Supplementary Comments of the Marine Spill Response Corporation to
           the Advance Notice of Proposed Rulemaking on Vessel Response Plans
           and Discharge-Removal Equipment, CGD 91-034/CGD 90-068

Dear Sir:

    Representatives of the Marine Spill Response Corporation ("MSRC") have
appreciated the opportunity to attend the various public meetings the Coast Guard
has hosted on tank vessel response plans and the carriage and inspection of discharge-
removal equipment. MSRC takes this opportunity to provide additional information
regarding the questions the Coast Guard has raised for further comment.

                        Sincerely,

                        John D. Costello

172

1350 I Street, NW Suite 300 Washington, DC 20005 Telephone 202 408 5700 Fax 202 371 0401

MSRC SUPPLEMENTAL COMMENTS ON
VESSEL RESPONSE PLAN ISSUES

The following comments address two issues for which the Coast Guard has requested further comment.

I. DEFINING RESPONSE TO THE "MAXIMUM EXTENT PRACTICABLE" AND ADVERSE WEATHER

MSRC is in the process of implementing plans to substantially increase oil spill response capability in United States coastal, tidal and certain other waters. MSRC's plans were developed based on a 30,000-ton spill scenario in the offshore environment. To identify the specific equipment and other capability, MSRC used the Delphi method, assembling expert consultants to develop and apply planning assumptions--a method not unlike what the Coast Guard is now undertaking to implement the regulations for vessel response plan requirements of the Oil Pollution Act of 1990 ("OPA 90"). MSRC believes that these planning efforts relate directly to the issues raised by the Coast Guard in its efforts to define "maximum extent practicable" response.

OPA 90 requires that vessels have response plans that ensure by contract or other approved means the capability to respond to a worst case discharge to the "maximum extent practicable." See OPA 90 § 4202. In essence, this requirement establishes the level of private response capability that the owner or operator of a vessel must have available and be able to manage to continue to transport oil.

In its various papers addressing the definition of the term "maximum extent practicable," the Coast Guard has proposed to objectively define this term through various planning factors to arrive at an acceptable quantity, quality and location of equipment, personnel and other resources. We believe this approach is appropriate, and should satisfy Congress' intent in OPA 90 to require credible planning and the private resources for response to large-scale spills and also provide an objective means for vessel owners and operators to evaluate response contractors' capabilities to meet owner and operator response obligations.

A. Use "planning assumptions"-- not "performance standards"

MSRC necessarily had to use various "planning assumptions" to develop the quantity and type of response equipment for its plans. The Coast Guard likewise is examining various planning factors. As stated in its paper on the definition of maximum extent practicable, "any standards and measurements established must be viewed strictly as planning standards, not performance standards."

192

MSRC agrees that performance standards, in the emergency response setting of an oil spill, are unwise, unworkable and misleading, because they create unrealistic expectations for future spills. Any one planning factor can vary substantially in any given spill, because of factors beyond the control of the response organizations, including, but not limited to, the characteristics of the oil, changing weather, location of the spill, oceanographic conditions, time of occurrence, condition of the damaged vessel, presence of debris, and regulatory requirements, to name but a few. Any individual factor may vary, but reasonable midpoint assumptions for each factor can produce a reasonable equipment inventory with an appropriate mix of response tools. In an actual spill event, those assets can only be applied to that particular spill using a reasonable best effort considering all the circumstances. Individual planning assumptions therefore should not be given greater weight than they deserve. In fact, they should not be called "standards" at all--only assumptions and factors used to develop and justify the level of capability required. That capability specification should consist of three elements: (1) an equipment system requirement; (2) a location requirement for that equipment; and (3) a mobilization requirement.

B.   Develop nationwide factors supplemented through the area planning process to take account of local or area variations

The Coast Guard asks whether it should establish planning factors that are consistent nationwide, with adjustments to be made for local conditions in the area planning process. MSRC used a similar approach. Consistent, nationwide planning factors, such as for "adverse weather," can produce a uniform standard for basic mechanical recovery and removal capability. It will also allow the Coast Guard to evaluate contractor response capability nationwide on a consistent basis. Area Planning Committees, which will have detailed knowledge of the conditions of a particular area, can take local variations into account to adjust, if needed, the capability provided by the basic nationwide standard. National response organizations like MSRC should be evaluated first against national criteria to determine the amount of capability for which they will be credited. Regional planning would evaluate only those factors special or unique to the local area to determine if additional capabilities are needed to meet special local needs.

Each of MSRC's five regional response centers is being equipped with mechanical response and removal capability based on a spill scenario of about 200,000 barrels (i.e., approximately 30,000 tons) in the offshore environment. This planning level roughly equates to a Valdez-size spill, the largest vessel spill ever to occur in the United States. It should be noted, however, that the majority of MSRC equipment has application in the less demanding environs of port and inland areas as well. MSRC's nationwide organization will allow it to cascade equipment and personnel from one region to another to supplement some of a region's resident capability.

193

The Coast Guard could adopt a similar approach. It could require mechanical recovery and removal equipment systems based on national planning factors for an initial best effort response to a 30,000 ton spill. Area Planning Committees, through the Area Contingency Plans ("ACPs"), could modify this equipment system capability based on local conditions. Any requirements for non-mechanical response capability should be linked to expedited decisionmaking with regard to use of dispersants and other non-mechanical spill mitigating substances and devices. The Area Planning Committees would also address the need for local and regional decisionmaking regarding tradeoffs, such as disposal of the volume of oily wastes that would result from mechanical recovery capability as compared with various non-mechanical approaches.

The authorization for use of non-mechanical response options must be clear, quickly arrived at and unequivocal. Dispersants are most effectively deployed by aircraft on a regional basis that may extend beyond the boundary of a single area. Thus, approval for dispersant use should be examined and resolved on a regional basis. This might appropriately be included in the Regional Contingency Plans. In addition, the ACPs should provide for approval of other non-mechanical response options and cite the decisions made on a regional basis regarding dispersant use as well. The ACPs should reflect the consensus of the federal, state and local agencies for when alternative response options (1) are preapproved, (2) are prohibited, and (3) require expedited decisionmaking to be used. Dispersant and other non-mechanical response capability thus should be incorporated into the Regional Contingency Plans and ACPs, where appropriate, to ensure proper approval for use.

The response community should not be required to have availability of dispersants and dispersant application equipment unless the government authorizes their use. The same is true for in situ burning equipment and bioremediants. In each case, the investment in terms of financial and manpower resources for stockpiling, training and maintenance would be wasted if the opportunity to use the option is foreclosed because of lack of timely approval.

C.   Specific planning factors

1.   Equipment capability in adverse weather

One of the Coast Guard's proposed planning factors relates to the "adverse weather" conditions that determine the type of equipment that may be counted towards meeting the required response capacity. MSRC also based its inventory on the performance of currently available equipment considering various sea states. This approach was designed to select response equipment capable of operating within a reasonable range of less than ideal weather conditions.

194

DOCUMENT 7-B

Appendix 1 to the letter: Comments of the Marine Spill Response Corporation to the Notice of Proposed Rulemaking, Table Marine Spill Response Corporation, Major Pollution Response Equipment List, and Table Sea State Definitions.

APPENDIX I - MSRC SUPPLEMENTARY COMMENTS

Pollution Response Equipment

Skimmer Capability and Limits

[NOTE: MSRC's equipment inventory was developed
through a multi-phased process. In addition to
applying in-house experience and knowledge, MSRC used
the Delphi approach, incorporating the advice and
recommendations from many knowledgeable sources
including the oil industry, ITOPF, Aleyeska, OSSC in
Southampton, NOFI, USCG, MMS, cooperatives and
contractors.]

INFORMATION PROVIDED HEREIN INVOLVES ASSUMPTIONS MADE
SOLELY FOR PLANNING PURPOSES AND DOES NOT REFLECT
PREDICTED ACTUAL PERFORMANCE IN ANY PARTICULAR SPILL
EVENT. NOTHING IN THIS INFORMATION IS INTENDED OR
SHOULD BE INTERPRETED AS A PROMISE OR STANDARD OF
PERFORMANCE.

MARINE SPILL RESPONSE CORPORATION

MAJOR POLLUTION RESPONSE EQUIPMENT LIST

1/22/92

	MANUFACTURER	NO.	TYPE	MFR'S Name Plate CAPACITY	SEA* STATE	OIL TYPE LIGHT	MEDIUM	HEAVY	OPERATING ENVIRONMENT CALM	HARBOR	OFFSHORE
SKIMMERS	Transrec 350 / Oil Trawl	16	Weir/Disk	2200 BPH	6	X	X	X	X	X	X
	Vikoma 3 Weir Boom	10	Boom Skimmer	1180 BPH	4	X	X	X	X	X	X
	Walosep W-4	12	Weir Vortex	740 BPH	5	X	X	-	X	X	X
	WP-1-30	8	Drum Separator	630 BPH	4	X	X	X	X	X	X
	Desmi Ocean	10	Weir	570 BPH	4	X	X	X	X	X	X
	GT-185	40	Weir	285 BPH	4-5	X	X	X	X	X	X
	Rope Mop	20	Rope	20 BPH	4	X	X	X	X	X	X
	Seawolf	2	Disc / Grab	NA	3	X	X	X	X	X	X
	Aard Vac 800	30	Section / Weir	800 BPH	3	X	X	-	X	X	-
PUMPS	MARCO Class XI Belt	10	Belt	150 BPH	3-4	X	X	X	X	X	X
	Eureka CCN-150	7	Centrifugal Archimedes	3000 BPH	-	HIGH CAPACITY			X	X	X
	DOP-250	58	Screw	690 BPH	-	HIGH VISCOSITY			X	X	X
BOOMS	Offshore 23/44	71,200 ft.	Curtain	-	5	X	X	X	X	X	X
	Med. Wt.	145,000 ft.	Rapid Deployment	-	4	X	X	X	X	X	X
	Slickbar Marine	145,000 ft.	Fence	-	4	X	X	X	X	X	X
	Beach Boom	108,000 ft.	Tidal Seal	-	2	X	X	X	X	X	-

* See Attached Definitions

INFORMATION PROVIDED HEREIN INVOLVES ASSUMPTIONS MADE SOLELY FOR PLANNING PURPOSES AND DOES NOT REFLECT PREDICTED ACTUAL PERFORMANCE IN ANY PARTICULAR SPILL EVENT. NOTHING IN THIS INFORMATION IS INTENDED OR SHOULD BE INTERPRETED AS A PROMISE OR STANDARD OF PERFORMANCE.

SEA STATE DEFINITIONS

2. Light breeze, 4 - 6 knots, small wavelets, crests of glassy appearance, not breaking.

3. Gentle breeze, 7 - 10 knots, large wavelets, crests begin to break, scattered white caps.

4. Moderate breeze, 11 - 16 knots, small waves 1.5 - 4 feet high, numerous white caps.

5. Fresh breeze, 17 - 21 knots, moderate waves 4 - 8 feet high, taking longer form, many white caps.

6. Strong breeze, 22 - 27 knots, with large waves 8 - 13 feet forming, white caps everywhere and spray.

DOCUMENT 8

Letter: Supplementary Comments of the Marine Spill Response Corporation to the Advance Notice of Proposed Rulemaking on Vessel Response Plans and Discharge-Removal Equipment. CGD 91-034/CGD 90-068 sent on July 30, 1992 by the Marine Spill Response Corporation ("MSRC") to the Executive Secretary Marine Safety Council and pages from 1 to 4 (on a total of 15) of the enclosed document: Comments to the Notice of Proposed Rulemaking, Vessel Response Plans.

MSRC
Marine Spill Response Corporation

JOHN D. COSTELLO
PRESIDENT

July 30, 1992

Executive Secretary
Marine Safety Council
(G-LRA-2/3406)
(CGD 91-034)
U.S. Coast Guard Headquarters
2100 Second Street, S.W.
Washington, D.C. 20593-0001

      Re: Comments of the Marine Spill Response Corporation to the Notice of
            Proposed Rulemaking, CGD 91-034

Dear Sir:

    The Marine Spill Response Corporation ("MSRC") appreciates this opportunity to comment on the Coast Guard's Notice of Proposed Rulemaking ("NPRM") on vessel response plans. 57 Fed. Reg. 27,514 (June 19, 1992).

    As a participant on the Oil Spill Response Negotiated Rulemaking Committee ("Reg Neg Committee"), and as a signatory to the Committee Agreement, MSRC supports those portions of the proposal expressed in the NPRM that reflect the Committee Agreement. MSRC's substantive comments regarding the current NPRM are limited in accordance with the Committee Agreement.

    We hope that the enclosed comments will be helpful to the Coast Guard as it continues to craft the vessel response plan regulations. We would be pleased to provide further elaboration on our comments should the Coast Guard have any questions regarding them.

                    Sincerely,

                    John D. Costello

Enclosure

MARINE SPILL RESPONSE CORPORATION
COMMENTS TO THE NOTICE OF PROPOSED RULEMAKING
Vessel Response Plans
57 Fed. Reg. 27,514 (June 19, 1992); CGD 91-034

MSRC is pleased to have this opportunity to comment on the Coast Guard's Notice of Proposed Rulemaking ("NPRM") on vessel response plans. As a participant on the Oil Spill Response Negotiated Rulemaking Committee ("Reg Neg Committee"), and as a signatory to the Committee Agreement, MSRC supports completely those portions of the proposal expressed in the NPRM that reflect the Committee Agreement. In accordance with the Committee Agreement, MSRC's substantive comments regarding the current NPRM are directed to those areas in which the NPRM covers issues that were not the subject of negotiations, where there is more than one option with respect to a particular issue, where consensus was not reached by the Committee, or where the NPRM does not appear to have the same substance and effect as that expressed in the Final Reports that constitute the Committee Agreement.

In addition, in response to the Coast Guard's request, these comments are structured according to the NPRM version of the proposed rule and accompanying discussion of proposed provisions (i.e., proposed preamble). Hence, the comments below indicate the particular section of the proposed rule to which they relate. They also combine MSRC's comments on the preamble discussion of the particular section with our comments on the language of the actual proposal for the particular section.

1.   SECTION 155.1010 - PURPOSE - The Vessel Response Plan Rule Should Not Establish Performance Standards

This section clarifies that the purpose of the proposed regulations is to affect planning for oil spill response. MSRC strongly supports the Coast Guard's clarification in the preamble and in the language of the proposed rule that "the requirements set forth in the rule are for planning purposes only and are not intended as performance standards." 57 Fed. Reg. at 27,516. MSRC agrees that performance standards, in the emergency response setting of an oil spill, are unworkable, unwise and misleading, because they create unrealistic expectations for response. Planning factors include a host of stated and unstated assumptions. Each planning factor can vary substantially in any given spill, because the factors represent a gross simplification of complex elements, many of which are beyond the control of response organizations. Although any individual factor may vary in an actual spill, appropriate assumptions for each factor, together with sound professional judgment, can produce an equipment inventory with a reasonable mix of response tools. In an actual spill event, those assets can only be applied to that particular spill using a reasonable best effort considering all the circumstances.

204

In spite of the Coast Guard's intent to avoid establishing standards for spill response performance, there are a few instances in which the language used in the proposed rule or preamble might be interpreted as such. We identify several of these instances as we comment on the particular sections below and encourage the Coast Guard to adopt unequivocal non-performance standard language in all places in the vessel response plan rule.

2.   SECTION 155.1015 - APPLICABILITY - The Coast Guard Should Clarify that the Requirements for Vessels Carrying Oil as Secondary Cargo Apply to Dedicated Response Vessels Carrying Oil Only Outside the Response Area

In the "applicability" section of the proposed preamble, the Coast Guard appropriately recognizes that dedicated response vessels should be exempt from response planning requirements while they conduct response-related carriage of oil within a response area.[1]/ See 57 Fed. Reg. at 27,538 (proposed section 155.1015); id. at 27,516 (proposed preamble). However, this section does not indicate that the applicable response planning requirements for dedicated response vessels carrying oil outside the response area would be only those for vessels carrying oil as secondary cargo, rather than for vessels carrying oil as primary cargo. Similarly, the proposed definition of "vessels carrying oil as secondary cargo" also does not indicate that dedicated response vessels would be such vessels. See 57 Fed. Reg. at 27,539 (proposed definition in section 155.1020); id. at 27,518 (proposed preamble). Thus, these two sections fail to implement the Reg Neg Committee Agreement, in which it was determined that the response planning requirements for secondary cargo vessels are more appropriate than those for primary cargo vessels for vessels dedicated to response. See Reg Neg Committee Agreement, Final Report-Applicability of Requirements to Various Type Tank Vessels, at 5-11 (March 27, 1992).

At two other points in the proposal, the Coast Guard has clearly reflected the Reg Neg Committee Agreement. However, these provisions do not appear to provide the necessary and unambiguous authority to remedy the problem. At the first point, the proposed preamble, in the section discussing substantive requirements for vessels that carry oil as secondary cargo, states that the requirements for vessels carrying oil as secondary cargo are intended to be applicable to dedicated response vessels carrying oil outside the response area. See 57 Fed. Reg. at 27,522. However, this statement is not

---

1/ As the Coast Guard notes in the proposed preamble, "requiring such vessels to have their own response plans could result in fewer such resources being available and would be contrary to the purpose and intent of OPA 90 to improve capability." 57 Fed. Reg. at 27,516.

evidenced by an explicit provision in the proposed rule.[2] Second, although the proposed rule and accompanying preamble at a different point state that "the response plan for a dedicated response vessel operating outside the response area must follow the same format as that for a vessel carrying oil as secondary cargo," they do not state that the substantive requirements for secondary cargo vessels apply. See 57 Fed. Reg. at 27,540 (proposed section 155.1030(e), emphasis added); see also id. at 27,520 (proposed preamble). Hence, MSRC is concerned that these clarifications may not carry the necessary legal authority to accomplish the intended and appropriate effect.

To make it absolutely clear and to provide the necessary legal support that dedicated response vessels are subject only to the planning requirements for secondary cargo vessels when carrying oil outside the response area, clarification should be made in the "applicability" section and the definition section, both in the preamble and the rule language. In addition, the rule language in Section 155.1030(e) should be revised to state that not only must the response plan for dedicated response vessels operating outside the response area follow the same format as vessels carrying oil as secondary cargo, but that the substantive requirements apply to such vessels as well. Otherwise, the provision might be subject to challenge or improperly interpreted to require dedicated response vessels carrying oil outside a response area to meet response planning requirements for vessels carrying oil as primary cargo, an interpretation that would be unnecessary and counterproductive, as well as contrary to the negotiated agreement.

3.   SECTION 155.1020 - DEFINITIONS

   a.   The definition of "cargo" should be revised to better accommodate oil spill response

As a means of effectuating the appropriate exemption of response vessels from response planning requirements, the Coast Guard has proposed to exclude oil recovered and handled within the response area from the definition of "cargo." See 57 Fed. Reg. at 27,538. However, the Coast Guard has stated that this exclusion would only apply to such oil recovered by response vessels used for the "emergency recovery of oil." Id. While all oil spills generally will be emergencies, there may be a reason to distinguish the phase of a spill response that is most urgent (i.e., an "emergency") from less urgent, though necessary, longer term phases of any particular response. Thus, use of the qualifying term "emergency" could have the effect of rendering response plan requirements applicable to response vessels upon the termination of the "emergency"

2/ The accompanying section of the rule does not reflect the statement made in the preamble applying the secondary cargo requirements to dedicated response vessels. See 57 Fed. Reg. at 27,544-545 (proposed section 155.1045).

phase, even though some on-water recovery is still necessary. MSRC notes that many of its future clients already categorize their responses into several phases with the "emergency" or initial phase being just one of them. Thus, the potential for misunderstanding the wording of the proposed rule already exists. In addition, use of the term "emergency" could preclude the availability of response vessels for drills or research spills that might in the future involve the approved release of oil. Hence, the Coast Guard should delete the term "emergency" from the cargo definition to avoid these unnecessary and potentially counterproductive results.

     b.   The definition of "contract or other approved means" should be clarified to avoid implication of performance standards

The proposed rule rightly reflects the Reg Neg Agreement that the vessel response plan rules are not intended to establish spill cleanup performance standards. However, as currently proposed, the definition of "contract or other approved means," (i.e., the means by which a vessel can demonstrate its compliance with response resource requirements) does not clearly reflect this intent. The definition specifies that the equipment and personnel must be available "within stipulated response times in specified geographic areas." 57 Fed. Reg. at 27,538 (proposed rule). The Coast Guard should clarify that this is meant to be directed to the <u>capability</u> of meeting the response times under a standard set of assumptions, and not interpreted to require that the response resources must meet the specified response times as performance standards.

     c.   The definition of "response area" should clearly include the entire area or areas where oil response activities may be undertaken

The Coast Guard has proposed to define "response area" in terms of the Captain of the Port ("COTP") zone or zones or a planning area within those zone(s). See 57 Fed. Reg. at 27,539 (proposed rule). Although on its face this differs from what the Reg Neg Committee agreed to, which was to define the response area only in terms of COTP zones or sectors,[3] MSRC does not object to the Coast Guard's amendment as long as the final rule recognizes that a "response area" may not be limited to a single COTP zone or single planning area within that zone.

The currently proposed definition of "response area" partially addresses the need to ensure that the area not be artificially circumscribed by geographic boundaries in that it recognizes that the area may include more than one COTP zone. However, it should be further clarified to state that a "response area" can include more than one planning

---

   3/ <u>See</u> Reg Neg Committee Agreement, Final Report-Applicability of Requirements to Various Type Tank Vessels, at 5-9.

DOCUMENT 9

Istituto Nazionale per Studi ed Esperienze di Architettura Navale (INSEAN) (Italian National Institute for Naval Architecture Studies and Experiences), Report No. 1/P.2201: Front page, table Channel Calibration Test, and table Oil Recovery Tests.

INSCAN

ROMA

ISTITUTO NAZIONALE PER STUDI ED ESPERIENZE DI ARCHITETTURA NAVALE

REPORT No. **1/P2201**

Tests No. **1^ - 2^**

MODEL HULL No. **P.2201**

MODEL SCREW No. **-**

SCALE RATIO **1:1**

CUSTOMER : Apram s.r.l. - Roma

SYSTEM : Skimmer

Rome, 5 novembre 1991

TEST BRANCH DIRECTOR

DIRECTOR

PRESIDENT

CHANNEL CALIBRATION TESTS

FILE P.2201   **TEST No. 1**

PRINCIPAL DATA

Speed course length —————— = 4,0 m —

Linear Regression results:

$Np = a + b \cdot Vm$

Coefficient a	0
Coefficient b	448,89
Standard deviation	12,96
Square Linear-correlation coefficient	0,99
N. of Sample	4
Degrees of freedom	3

Np (r.p.m.)	Δtm (s)	Vm (m/s)	Vm (kts)
200	17,1	0,23	0,45
300	12,5	0,32	0,62
400	8,7	0,46	0,89
605	5,7	0,70	1,36

Vm (kts) (interpolated values)	Np (r.p.m.)
0,40	180
0,50	224
0,60	269
0,70	314
0,80	359
0,90	404
1,00	449
1,10	494
1,20	539
1,30	584
1,40	628
1,50	673
1,60	718

I.N.S.E.A.N.

ROME 4.6.91

Straight Line speed–number of rev.
(interpolation)

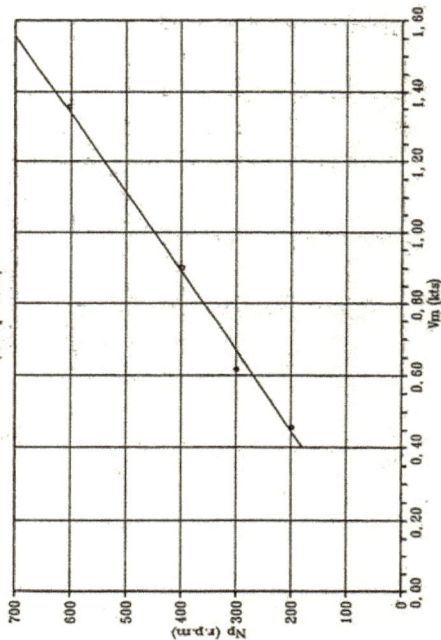

NOTE   1

Np = number of revolutions of the channel screw propeller

Vm = superficial average speed

212

OIL RECOVERY TESTS FILE P.2201   TEST No. 2

I.N.S.E.A.N.

CALCULUS DATA

$$Np = 448.8852 \cdot Vm$$
$$Qo+w = Kp \cdot No+w$$
$$Qw = Kp \cdot Nw$$
$$RE = (Qo+w - Qw)/Qo+w$$
$$ORR = Qo+w - Qw$$
$$E1 = RE \%$$

Scale ratio	1,0	—
IFO 180 Oil viscosity	1,8000	$^*10\text{-}4\ m^2/sec$
IFO 180 oil density	97,47	$Kg \cdot sec^2/m^{-4}$
Oil+water Viscosity (2)	494,6000	$^*10\text{-}4\ m^2/sec$
Oil+water Density (2)	100,45	$Kg \cdot sec^2/m^{-4}$
Drum's Diameter	0,637	m
Drum's angular velocity	29	r.p.m.
Drum's tangential velocity	0,97	m/s (1.88 kts)
Intake height	0,004	m
Intake breadth	1,350	m

Meas. n	Vm (kts)	Np (r.p.m.)	No+w (r.p.m.)	Nw (r.p.m.)	Qo+w (m3/h)	Qw (m3/h)	RE	ORR (m3/h)
1	0,82	370	263	46	13,9	2,4	0,83	11,5
2	0,82	370	515	145	27,3	7,7	0,72	19,6
3	0,82	370	413	76	21,9	4,0	0,82	17,9
4	1,01	453	350	60	18,6	3,2	0,83	15,4
5	1,01	453	385	35	20,4	1,9	0,91	18,6
6	1,01	453	490	95	26,0	5,0	0,81	20,9
7	1,25	563	330	65	17,5	3,4	0,80	14,0
8	1,25	563	528	120	28,0	6,4	0,77	21,6
9	1,25	563	240	48	12,7	2,5	0,80	10,2
10	1,54	690	325	58	17,2	3,1	0,82	14,2
11	1,54	690	496	70	26,3	3,7	0,86	22,6

ROME 4.6.91

EFFICIENCY OF THE RECOVERY SYSTEM
(tested values)

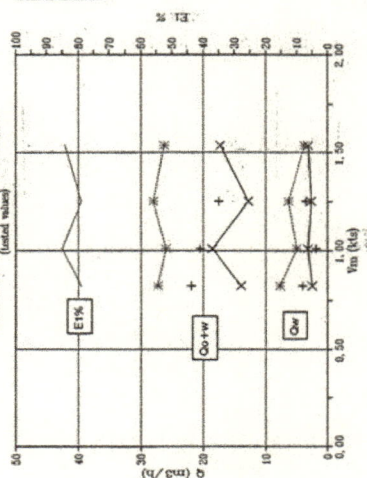

E1 %

Qo+w

Qw

* Qmin
+ Qmean
* Qmax

NOTE   2

$$E1 = \frac{\text{Oil recovery amount}}{\text{Total fluid recovery amount}}\ \%$$

(1) environmental temperature during tests t = 16°C
(2) measured values on a sample drawn at the test end at 16°C

Np = number of revolutions of the channeled screw propeller
Vm = speed of advance
No+w = number of revolutions of the oil+water recovery pump
Nw = number of revolutions of the water recirculating pump
Qo+w = delivery of the oil+water recovery pump
Qw = delivery of the water recirculating pump
Kp =   0,053

DOCUMENT 10

Lloyd's Register, Certificate No. NAP 100334/1.

Lloyd's Register

Project: —

Certificate No.: **NAP 100334/1**

Client: **Messrs. APRAM srl**

Office: **NAPLES**

Client's Order No.: **APRAM letter dd. 11.4.91**

Date: **18.10.1991**

Order Status: **COMPLETE**

Inspection dates
First: **04.06.91**

Final: **17.10.91**

This is to certify that the undersigned Surveyor to this Society did attend on the 4th June 1991 at request of Messrs. APRAM srl at the Works of Messrs. S.V.M.-Via Naide 46-ROMA for the purpose of examining and testing the "Skimmer" machine, suitably designed and made to recover oil from the sea surface.

All tests have been carried out as follows :

- by means of a water circulating tank.
- in accordance with APRAM Dwg. N°6.
- in presence of Italian official certification body "I.N.S.E.A.N."
- results reported on I.N.S.E.A.N. official form N° "P2201" dd. 16.07.91.
-

The oil recovery efficiency has been found from 0,72 to 0,91 and the oil recovery rate value found from 10,2 to 22,6 m^3/h, therefore, the skimmer is considered working with satisfactory results.

END

G. PAZZANO
Surveyor to Lloyd's Register

DOCUMENT 11

Stazione Sperimentale per i Combustibili (Experimental Station for Fuels), Certificate N. B19879.

STAZIONE SPERIMENTALE PER I COMBUSTIBILI

Viale A. De Gasperi 3
20097 San Donato Milanese MI
Tel. 02/510031 Fax 514286 Telex 321622

19/07/91

CERTIFICATO N. B19879

ANALISI DI UN CAMPIONE DICHIARATO: EMULSIONE IFO 180-ACQUA
DAL COMMITTENTE: APRAM - ROMA
ARRIVATO IL: 09/07/91   RICHIESTA DEL: 04/07/91
RIFERIMENTO:
                                                  (ns.rif.2570)

CONDIZIONI DEL CAMPIONE: contenuto in barattolo di vetro.

RISULTATI

ACQUA	ASTM D 95	65	% peso
VISCOSITA'			
a 50 °C		3180	cSt
a 16 °C		49460	cSt

La viscosità e' stata determinata mediante viscosimetro
rotazionale CONTRAVES RHEOMAT 135.

IL CAPO LABORATORIO ANALISI
Dr. A. Galtieri

IL DIRETTORE
Prof. A. Fiumara

221

DOCUMENT 12

Certificate Prot. 7655: Maritime Compartment of Civitavecchia
The ship's captain (CP) head of the Maritime Compartment and Commander of the Civitavecchia Harbour, declares that official documents certify that Mr. Giuseppe Ayroldi has performed n. 6 (six) tests and public demonstrations inside the harbour of Civitavecchia with the "Perseus" skimmer.
Each test, performed under the direct control of this Maritime Compartment, always ended with the removal of all the oily material purposely poured onto the sea, leaving the test area absolutely free of polluting residues.

LIRE 100
MARCA DA BOLLO
LIRE 100
L.500

<u>CAPITANERIA DI PORTO DI CIVITAVECCHIA</u>   Prot. 7655

Il Capitano di Vascello(CP), Capo del Compartimento

Marittimo e Comandante del Porto di Civitavecchia;

-VISTA l'istanza avanzata in data 12.6.75 dal Signor

Giuseppe Ayroldi, residente in Roma,P.za Mincio 4;

================C E R T I F I C A===============

CHE DAGLI ATTI D'UFFICIO RISULTA che il Sig.Giuseppe

Ayroldi ha effettuato con lo skimmer "Perseus", nell'in

terno del Porto di Civitavecchia, n.6 (sei)Fra prove

e dimostrazioni pubbliche;

Ciascuna prova, svolta sotto il diretto controllo

di questa Capitaneria si é conclusa sempre con il

recupero di tutto il materiale oleoso appositamente

versato in mare, lasciando il luogo della prova

assolutamente sgombro di residui inquinanti.- =======

Si rilascia il presente certificato per i soli usi

consentiti dalla legge. ===========================

Civitavecchia, lì 16.6.1975   p. IL COMANDANTE
                                     Capitano di Vascello(CP)
                                       (Antonino DI BETTA)

                                     IL COMANDANTE IN II

225

DOCUMENT 13

Letter *Subject: Apram Co. - Offer of Antipollution Vessels* sent on October 20, 1993 by the head of the Technical Inspectorate (I.T.) of the Ministry for the Merchant Navy to the Office of the Minister and, c. c., to the Central Inspectorate for the Defence of the sea: *This letter follows the previous note of October 25, 1993 on the subject, and advises that the Apram Company has sent to this I.T. documentation relating to tests carried out by INSEAN and the Lloyd's Register on the skimmer and the model of the antipollution vessel (a total of 3 reports) owned by the Company.*
The tests results demonstrate that the said means and equipment work in positive manner.

Ministero della Marina Mercantile
ISPETTORATO TECNICO

MINISTERO
DELLA MARINA MERCANTILE

0 2 NOV. 1993

N° 253K

Roma, 2 9 OTT. 1993 19

All'Ufficio di Gabinetto

——————— SEDE ———————

Divisione _____ Sez. _____
Prot. N° 7|25|28'3 Allegati ___

Risposta al Foglio del
Div. _____ Sez. _____ N° _____

OGGETTO: Soc. APRAM - Offerta di mezzi nautici disinquinan-
ti.

e, p.c. All'Ispettorato Centrale
per la Difesa del Mare
- SEDE -

Si fa seguito alla precedente nota del 25 ottobre 1993
all'argomento per comunicare che la Soc. APRAM ha fatto pervenire a
questo I.T. una documentazione relativa a prove eseguite dall'INSEAN
e dal Lloyd Register of Shipping sullo skimmer e sul modello di nave
disinquinante (complessivamente 3 prove) di proprietà della Società.
I risultati delle prove dimostrano che detti mezzi e
attrezzature funzionano in maniera positiva.

Il Capo
dell'Ispettorato Tecnico

d3/carr/p.72

229

DOCUMENT 14

The European Community Commission, Directorate General for Environment, Consumer Protection and Nuclear Safety, letter of transmission of the contract having as its object *Recovery of Heavy Oils in the High Seas.*

**COMMISSION
DES
COMMUNAUTES EUROPEENNES**

Direction générale de l'environnement,
de la protection des consommateurs
et de la sécurité nucléaire.

Bruxelles............. le ...

Monsieur G. AYROLDI

APRAM SRL

Via Guido Zanobini, 55

I. 00175 ROMA

Monsieur,

Je vous prie de bien vouloir trouver, ci-joint, un exemplaire du
contrat ayant pour objet la " Récupération d'huiles lourdes en haute
mer ".

dûment signé et destiné à vos archives.

D'autre part, je vous informe que le nécessaire a été fait pour le
premier paiement comme indiqué à l'article 4 du contrat.

Je vous prie d'agréer, Monsieur,　　　　l'expression de mes sen-
timents les meilleurs.

A. ANDREOPOULOS
Directeur Général

Annexe

DOCUMENT 15

Certificate of Incorporation of Endtech, Environmental Technologies, Inc. (First page)

CERTIFICATE OF INCORPORATION

OF

ENVIRONMENTAL DEFENSE TECHNOLOGIES, INC.

FIRST: The name of the Corporation is Environmental Defense Technologies, Inc.

SECOND: The address of the Corporation's initial registered office in Delaware and the name of the Corporation's initial registered agent at such address are as follows:

> The Corporation Trust Company
> 1209 Orange Street
> New Castle County
> Wilmington, Delaware

THIRD: The purpose for which the Corporation is formed is to engage in any lawful act or activity for which corporations may be organized under the General Corporation Law of Delaware.

FOURTH: The total number of shares of stock which the Corporation is to have the authority to issue is 1,000 shares of common stock, all of a par value of ten cents ($.10) per share.

FIFTH: The name and mailing address of the incorporator are as follows:

> Gary W. Glisson
> Rogers & Wells
> 1737 H Street, N.W.
> Washington, D.C. 20006

SIXTH: In furtherance and not in limitation of the powers conferred by statute, the Directors of the Corporation

THE SOURCES

Giuseppe Ayroldi, *L'inquinamento d'oro, come si ruba – anche – sull'emergenza ambientale* (Golden pollution, how they steal—also—on environmental emergencies), Le Vespe, Gennaio 2010

Colin Crouch, *Post-Democracy*, Polity Press/UK, 2004

Bob Graham, William K. Reilly, Frances G. Beinecke, Donald F. Boesch, Terry D. Garcia, Cherry A. Murray, Fran Ulmer, *Deep Water, the Gulf Oil Disaster and the Future of Offshore Drilling – Report to the President.*

Vilfredo Pareto, *Trattato di sociologia* (Treaty of Sociology), Paravia, 1923

Paolo Mauro, *Corruption and composition of government expenditure*, The Journal of Public Economics, 1969

The Oil Pollution Act of 1990 (OPA'90) Public Law 101-380

Federal Register, Friday, August 30, 1991

International Convention for the Prevention of Pollution from Ships, as amended (MARPOL 73/78), London, 17 Feb. 1978;

United Nations Convention on the Law of the Sea (UNCLOS), Montego Bay, 16 Nov. 1964;

International Convention for the Prevention of the Sea by Oil (OILPOL);

International Convention on Oil Pollution Preparedness, Response and Control (OPRC), London, 30 Nov. 1990;

International Convention on Civil Liability for Oil Pollution Damage (CLC 1969), Brussels, 29 Nov. 1969;

Department of Transportation, U.S. Coast Guard, 33 CFR Part 155 (CGD 91-034/90-068) RIN 2115-AD81 and 68, *Vessel Response Plans and Carriage and Inspection of Discharge-Removal Equipment*, Federal Register/ Vol. 56, No. 169/ Friday, August 30, 1991;

National Resources Defense Council (NRDC), *Safety at Bay, A Review of Oil Spill Prevention and Cleanup in U.S. Waters*;

Department of Transportation/ Coast Guard/ 33 CFR Part 155/ Discharge Removal Equipment for Vessels carrying Oil/ Interim final rule. Federal Register/ Vol. 58, No 244/ Wednesday, December 22, 1993.

The White House, Office of the Press Secretary, *Remarks by the President in a Discussion on Jobs and the Economy in Charlotte*, North Carolina, April 2, 2010, http://www.whitehouse.gov;

House Subcommittee on Coast Guard and Navigation, *Hearing on the implementation of section 4202(a)(6) of the oil pollution act of 1990 requiring oil-carrying vessels to carry discharge response equipment*, February 17,

March 18, 1993, U.S. Government Printing Office, Washington D.C., 1993;

Golob's Oil Pollution Bulletin, October 23, 1992;

Federal Register, Vol. 59, No 126, Friday, July 1, 1994, Rules and Regulations;

ASTM International, *ASTM F 631 – 80 Standard Test Method for Full-Scale Advancing Oil Spill Removal Devices*;

OHMSETT, *Summary of U.S. Environmental Protection Agency's Ohmsett testing, 1974 – 1979*;

Galileo Galilei, *Discorsi e dimostrazioni matematiche sopra due nuove scienze*;

Holy Bible, *The Book of Genesis*;

ASTM, *A Century of Progress, Early Standard Development and the Origins of ASTM*;

Marine Spill Response Corporation, *MSRC Supplemental comments on vessel response plan issues* sent on January 27, 1991 to the Executive Secretary, Marine Safety Council, (G-LRA-2/3406), (CGD 91-034/CGD 90-068), U.S. Coast Guard Headquarters, 2100 Second Street, S.W., Washington D.C. 20593-0001;

Marine Spill Response Corporation, *Comments to the notice of proposed rulemaking* sent, on July 30, 1992,by MSRC To the Executive Secretary, Vessel Response Plans, 57 Fed. Reg. 27,514 (June 19, 1992); CGD 91-034 Marine Safety Council;

International Herald Tribune of May 12, 2010;

The Washington Post on-line edition, June 29, 2010;

Associated Press, the *glaring errors and omissions in BP's oil spill response plans*, Wednesday, June 09, 2010;

The paper "Oil Spill Commission Landmark Report on Gulf Disaster Proposes Urgent Reform of Industry and Government Practices to Overhaul U.S. Offshore Drilling Safety" released on January 11, 2011 11:00 a.m. EST

Wikipedia, the Columbia Accident Investigation Board (CAIB) (http://caib.nasa.gov/);

Oil & Gas Journal, May 10, 2010;

International Herald Tribune, May 28, 2010;

OIL POLLUTION ACT OF 1990 [As Amended Through P.L. 106–580, Dec. 29, 2000];

Woods Hole Oceanographic Institution News Release: *First Study of Dispersant in Gulf Spill Suggests a Prolonged Deepwater Fate*;

Latham, Mark A., *Five Thousand Feet and Below, The Failure to Adequately Regulate Deepwater Oil Production Technology*;

Albert Einstein, *On the movement of small particles suspended in a stationary liquid demanded by the molecular-kinetic theory of heat*;

Criminal Court of Naples, Criminal proceeding n. 1159/87 r.g.g.i., n. 9897/87 r.g.p.m.;

Proxy of Trieste, Verbal Questioning of Mr. Della Zonca Agostino, «*QUESTION OF SO-SAID MINISTRIAL BRIBES*»;

Criminal Court of Rome, Criminal proceeding n. 1047/97 R.G.P.M., n. 18/97 R.G. COLL.;

Criminal Court of Milan, criminal proceeding n. 8655/92 R.G. crime reports, Prison of San Vittore, Office of the Judge for Preliminary Investigations Mr. Italo Ghitti, *Verbal questioning of Mr. Roberto Ferraris, CEO of Castalia Company*;

Ministry of Merchant Marine, Minutes of the gathering of 7.9.87 of the Committee ex art. 8 of Law no. 979/82, page 4;

Guardia di Finanza (the Italian Financial Police), *Judicial Police report no. 41678/VII/1ª for the Court of Rome*;

Chamber of Commerce of Naples, copy of the "historic certificate" of the Castalia Company;

Study of Notary Luciano Fabiani of Rome, Minutes of the *Extraordinary Meeting held on December 10, 1987 by the Castalia Company* and recorded and filed with the Court and the Chamber of Commerce of Naples with the repertory n. 20804;

Criminal Court of Rome, criminal proceeding n. 1683/89G R.G.P.M., n. 41/89 R.G. COLL.;

Letter Protocol no. 7/25/1623 continuing on the subject: *Offers for services prevention and control of pollution of the sea* transmitted on May 18, 1987 by Eng. Umberto Sarno, Head of the Technical Inspectorate of the Ministry of the Merchant Navy, to the Central Inspectorate for the defense of the sea;

Court of Auditors, Resolution no. 65/93;

The Head of the Technical Inspectorate Eng. Umberto Sarno, Note protocol no. 7/25/4553 sent on October 26, 1987, to the Cabinet of the Minister, to the Central Inspectorate of the Sea Defense and to the Inspectorate General of Harbours;

Court of Genoa, Expert Judgment on the damages to the environment caused to the Gulf of Genoa by the explosion of the Supertanker Haven (as reported by the *Corriere della Sera*).

ACRONYMS

AA.GC	Affari Generali (General Affairs)
AC	Alternating current
ACP	Area Contingency Plan
ASTM	American Society for Testing and Materials
AUV	Autonomous Underwater Vehicle
BOP	Blow-Out Preventer
BP	BP (formerly known as British Petroleum)
BTEX	Benzene, Toluene, Ethybenzene, and total Xylenes
CEO	Chief Executive Officer
CERCLA	Comprehensive Environmental Response, Compensation, and Liability Act
CLC	International Convention on Civil Liability for Oil Pollution Damage
C.P.	Capitanerie di Porto
CWA	Clean Waters Act

GDP	Gross Domestic Product
CPR	Controlled Products Regulations
DOI	Department of the Interior
DOT	Department of Transportation
DSL	Domestic Substances List
ECB	European Central Bank
Reg. Neg. Committee	Oil Spill Response Negotiated Rulemaking Committee
EEC	European Economic Community
E.O.	Executive Order
EPA	Environmental Protection Agency
ET	External Tank
ICDM	Ispettorato Centrale Difesa Mare (Central Inspectorate for the Defense of Sea)
IMO	International Maritime Organization
INSEAN	Istituto Nazionale per Studi ed Esperienze di Architettura Navale (Italian National Institute for Naval Architecture Studies and Experiences)
ISO	International Organization for Standardization
IRI	Istituto per la Ricostruzione Industriale (Institute for Industrial Reconstruction)
I.T.	Ispettorato Tecnico (Technical Inspectorate)
MMS	Mineral Management Service
MPA	Marine Preservation Association
MSDS	Material Safety Data Sheet

MSRC	Marine Spill Response Corporation
NCP	National Oil and Hazardous substance Pollution Contingency Plan
NRDC	National Resources Defense Council
NWS	Naval Weapons Station
OHMSETT	Oil and Hazardous Materials Simulated Environmental Test Tank
OILPOL	International Convention for the Prevention of the Sea by Oil
OPA'90	Oil Pollution Act of 1990
OPRC	International Convention on Oil Pollution Preparedness, Response and Control
ORR	Oil Recovery Rate
OSHA	Occupational Safety and Health Administration
OSRVs	Oil Spill Response Vessels
P.A.	Pubblica Amministrazione (Public Administration)
RE	Oil Recovery Efficiency
R.G.G.I.,	Registro Generale Giudice Istruttore
R.G.P.M.	Registro Generale Pubblico Ministero
SEMP	Safety and Environmental Management Program
STARs	Spill Team Area Responders
TE	Throughput Efficiency
TPS	Thermal Protection System
TSCA	Toxic Substances Control Act
UC	University of California

USCG	United States Coast Guard
WHOI	Woods Hole Oceanographic Institution

INDEX OF NAMES

Ferraris, Roberto, 120, 120n, 242.
Ferraro, Renato, 122, 123.
Feynman, Richard, 68.
Freeman, James D., 113, 163.

G

Galilei, Galileo, 38, 42, 43, 43n, 121, 241.
Garcia Márquez, Gabriel, 93n.
Garcia, Terry D., 239.
Garofoli, Giovanni, 134.
Gerone, 38.
Ghitti, Italo, 120, 120n, 242.
Graber, Hans, 60, 61.
Graham, Bob, 239.
Gubaidullin, Marcel, 20.

H

Hayward, Tony, 13, 89, 90.
Hazen, Terry, 56n.
Higgs, Peter, 43.
Hofmeister, John, 56n.
Hogan & Hartson, 113, 163, 177.

J

Jindal, Bobby, 60.
Joule, James Prescott, 43.

K

Knowlton, Brian, 96.
Kaufman, Leslie, 55, 96.
Kepler, Johannes, 42.
Kido Soule, Melissa C., 103.
Kirby, David, 107.
Kraus, Karl, 7.
Krauss, Clifford, 96.

Kujawinski, Elizabeth B., 103, 104.

L

La Greca, Sebastiano, 134.
Latham, Mark A. 83, 85, 242.
Lener, Alfredo, 121.
Lush, Tamara, 59.

M

Mani, 189.
Maresca, Maria Francesca, 134.
Mauro, Eugenio, 134.
Mauro, Paolo, 239.
Maxwell, James Clerk, 43.
Mazzi, Manuela, 120n.
Mckinley, James, 55,96.
Mickey Mouse, 90.
Mohr, Holbrok, 59.
Morley, Bob, 9.
Morozov, Yury, 21.
Munchausen (Baron of), 69.
Murray, Cherry A., 239.

N

Nyholm, Allison, 55.

O

Obama, Barack, 13, 62, 65, 68, 75, 76. 86, 89, 90, 96.
Oersted, Hans Christian, 43.
Ostwald, Wilhelm, 110n.
Ott, Riki, 56n.

P

Pareto, Vilfredo, 239.
Perrin, Jean, 110n.

Pirro, Silvia, 134.
Plank, Max, 43.
Prandini, Giovanni, (Gianni), 14, 120, 121, 128, 130, 132.
Pritchard, Justin, 59.
Prodi, Romano, 119n, 127, 137.

R

Raphael (Raffaello, Sanzio), 121.
Rahal, Nick J., 85.
Reagan, Ronald, 60n.
Reilly, William K., 68, 239.
Risch, James E., 96.
Roos, Judith, 55, 56.
Rothwell & Brown, 113.

S

Saieva, Giuseppe, 134.
Saint Francis, 121.
Salazar, Ken, 60, 95, 92.
Santonastaso, Mauro, 126.
Santucci, Emidio, 125.
Sarno, Umberto, 124, 131, 133, 243.
Saulny, Susan, 96.
Schulze, Robert, 51, 53.
Scivicco, Aldo, 134.
Scott, David R., 43n.
Shaw, Susan, 108.
Skoloff, Brian, 59.
Spirito, Angelo, 120n, 123.
Sullivan, Eileen, 59.

T

Tauzin, Billy, 30, 32, 33, 42, 58, 68, 77, 90.
Thomson, Joseph John, 43.
Tito, Raffaele, 120n.
Touschek, Bruno, 44.
Trivellini, Antonio, 134.

U

Ulmer, Fran, 239.

V

Vacca Torelli, Marcello, 122, 123.
Vecchione, Salvatore, 134.
Virgil (Publius Vergilius Maro), 121.
Vizzini, Carlo, 120, 121, 132.
Volta, Alessandro, 43.

W

Wald, Mattew L., 96.
Watson, John, 11, 32, 74.
Watt, James, 60n, 87, 97.
Weber, Harry R., 59.

Y

Yaeger, Kevin M., 56n.
Yarnold, David, 19.

Z

Zucchini, Paolo, 128, 129, 130, 131, 132, 133, 134.